The Writer's Business Reference

About the Authors

MICHAEL E. FASSIOTTO has degrees from San Francisco State University and a Ph.D. from the University of Hawaii. An experienced editor and journalist, he teaches English and Communications at Chaminade University of Honolulu and has been recognized for teaching excellence from the University of Hawaii—West Oahu.

MELBA E. KOP is an Associate Professor in Communications at Chaminade University of Honolulu. A graduate of the University of Hawaii, she has been recognized for excellence in teaching by the Pacific Speech Association and Chaminade University and has many years of experience in the fields of interpersonal and public communication.

CAROLYN M. KURIYAMA has degrees from the University of Washington and Harvard University. She has served as a Program Coordinator of Executive Education at Harvard Business School and has had experience in developing small businesses. An award-winning teacher, she has taught at the University of Hawaii and Chaminade University.

ABOUT COMMUNICATE, INC.

Together, Fassiotto, Kop, and Kuriyama are the principal consultants for the Honolulu-based firm, *Communicate, Inc. Communicate, Inc.* designs and presents training programs in writing and speaking to businesses throughout the Pacific Basin. It also organizes and coordinates workshops and institutes for companies in Honolulu.

The Write Business Reference

Communicate, Inc.

Michael Fassiotto
Melba Kop
Carolyn Kuriyama

Out of print - per T/c 6/21/99 to
Prentice Hall

 1-800-922-0579-customer Service
1-800-526-0485-faculty copy

Prentice Hall
Upper Saddle River, NJ 07458

Library of Congress Cataloging-in-Publication Data
The write business reference / Communicate, Inc.
    p. cm.
   Includes index.
   ISBN 0–13–036708–7
   1. Commercial correspondence. I. Communicate, Inc.
HF5726.W76 1995
808'.06665—dc20   94-40700
                                        CIP

Acquisitions Editor: Elizabeth Sugg
Production Editors: Rose Kernan and Fred Dahl
Copy editor: Rose Kernan
Designer: Fred Dahl
Manufacturing Manager: Edward O'Dougherty

© 1995 by Prentice-Hall, Inc.
A Simon & Schuster Company
Upper Saddle River, New Jersey 07458

Printed in the United States of America

10 9   8   7   6   5 4 3 2

ISBN 0-13-036708-7

Prentice-Hall International (UK) Limited, *London*
Prentice-Hall of Australia Pty. Limited, *Sydney*
Prentice-Hall of Canada Inc., *Toronto*
Prentice-Hall Hispanoamericana, S.A., *Mexico*
Prentice-Hall of Japan, Inc., *Tokyo*
Simon & Schuster Asia Pte. Ltd., *Singapore*
Editora Prentice-Hall do Brasil, Ltda., *Rio de Janeiro*

Contents

Chapter 3

Writing Effective Reports, 29

Chapter 4

Correcting Grammar, 61

Chapter 5

Punctuating Properly, 71

Chapter 7
Using Words Correctly, 95

Chapter 8
Formatting Your Message, 113

About *The Write Business Reference*

A Note from *Larry W. Riggs*, Chairman
Department of Modern Languages
Butler University
Indianapolis, Indiana

I know from direct experience that, conceptually and practically, *The Write Business Reference* is an excellent book. I have used these materials and the approach they embody in seminars, workshops, and tutorials. Working alone with individual employees or public and private organizations, I have found that this approach enables people to identify problems in their writing quickly and clearly, and begin immediately to solve them. In workshops and seminars, working with the book's authors, I have regularly been amazed by results achieved in groups of military personnel and of public and private employees from every level of responsibility. The approach works, and people enjoy using it.

As a university professor and administrator, I constantly apply what I've learned from the authors in my own writing. I am a more effective and comfortable communicator than I was. I am also a better *teacher* of writing. My students benefit from the clarity, simplicity, and practicality of this approach.

I'm familiar with the process that produced *The Write Business Reference*. The authors have analyzed thousands of pages of actual organizational writing and reams of materials produced in seminars and workshops. No other book on the market so clearly focuses on writing as it actually functions in real systems of communication. I recommend *The Write Business Reference* with the greatest enthusiasm!

From *George Simpson*, Director
Center for Biographical Research
University of Hawaii
Honolulu, Hawaii

This book supports the need to communicate well in contemporary corporate culture. Three reasons for good communication are implicit in what Michael Fassiotto, Melba Kop, and Carolyn Kuriyama recommend and show: good writing has a dominant emotive attitude behind it; good writing presumes that the writer is conscious of his or her role in a real life setting; and good writing presumes that the outcome is action—physical, corporate, or mental.

First, the authors imply that in a corporate setting a dominant emotion favoring teamwork is essential. Their idiom for this attitude is "service." The overwhelming experience in America is the immigrant experience. The great success story of America is the way the immigrants met perils of the unknown by teamwork. The great premise of American corporate success is helping each other understand what's going on. Helping each other cannot be done without a positive attitude toward choosing words that foster teamwork. This book says in a very practical way, "play team even when the message is 'no.'"

Second, the authors imply that writers should be conscious of their roles—who they are in a given situation—when they communicate. In this book, the main role assumed for a good writer is that of a judicious person. The examples show that the boss is a reasonable boss, that the colleague is a straight shooter, that the subordinate wants to get the job done. The communication quarterback throws the communication ball in a tight catchable spiral. The communication end gathers it in and runs fast for the goal line. The communication guards and tackles protect good communication with skillful and resolute blocks against misapprehension. The authors make it clear that writers must feature themselves as people with judgment, people who can choose, and that is shown in this book on almost every page with the choices between formulations marked "yes" and those marked "no."

Third, the authors assume that good writing results in a worthwhile action, either physical, or organizational, or mental. Each of us lives in a different physical or organizational environment, which we try to cope with verbally, but when it comes to mental action our minds share a great deal. Almost all high cultures think of thought as action. Even when we are asleep, we experience the emotion, judgment, and action of dreams. But at the everyday workaday level, we sometimes forget that thought and language are action. Nothing activates good thought so much as a good or correct word, and nothing activates bad thoughts or no thought so much as a bad or incorrect word. Nothing shows this nowadays so much as our computers, those rough approximations of mind that send millions of tiny acts zooming down unseen silicon highways. A computer without action has a plug. This book, by example and precept, gently suggests that a writer who does not engender action has a pulled plug. Its point is that a writer must stimulate mental action so that the work can be done higher, faster, stronger. ...

You Must Read This Preface!

You are a careful writer (we know this because you bought this book), and you are a careful reader (we know this because you are reading the Preface). Careful writers and readers are always looking for ways to improve their skills. Therefore, this Preface offers you a few suggestions about using this book.

- *Browse through this book.* We won't feel hurt if you don't read it from cover to cover. Adults learn best when they receive information that they can apply at once. Therefore, before you start to write your next report, read Chapter 3—Writing Effective Reports—or when you are next ready to proofread, consider Chapter 9—Proofreading Carefully. If you want to get started right away, we suggest you read Chapters 1 and 2—Applying the Basic Principles of Writing and Organizing Your Letters and Memos. These two chapters contain the fundamental points on which the rest of the book is based.

- *Save your reference books. The Write Business Reference* is designed to be a *short* manual to help you out when you need help. It is not a complete reference. For example, we reduce comma usage to three basic rules (one of the references we consulted during the writing of this text lists over 33 rules for comma placement). So we advise you to keep a dictionary, a grammar text, and a thesaurus nearby when you are writing. They can help you answer any of the more tortuous problems you might run into.

- *Do one thing at a time.* We have found that many people who want to improve their writing skills try to do everything at once and end up doing very little. Be systematic. Make a list—if you like lists—of all the things you would like to change in your writing, but only work on *one* thing at a time. If, for example, you need to work on subject/verb agreement and organizing your letters, choose the one more important to you and concentrate only on that. When you have conquered that problem, then you can move to the second. You will find your journey to confident writing more successful when you take a single-step-at-a-time approach.

The Write Business Reference is *one* way to improve your writing. There are other ways to improve your writing, and we wouldn't argue with any of them. We have found, however, that this way works. It has been applied by thousands of professionals and students and they always tell us how well it works for them. We also have seen their results, so we can testify to its efficacy.

One last comment. We have had fun teaching the ideas expressed in this book, and almost as much fun writing it (writing is never an entirely fun job). We would like you to enjoy *The Write Business Reference* and, more importantly, enjoy the experience of writing on the job or at school.

Michael Fassiotto
Melba Kop
Carolyn Kuriyama
Honolulu, Hawaii

Acknowledgments

The list of people who helped us prepare this book is very long, and we appreciate and thank each of them. Several of our contributors, however, merit specific acknowledgment.

- All of our students and clients from whom we have learned what was important.
- Joseph Murray, the first person to realize *The Write Business Reference*'s potential.
- The staff at Prentice Hall for all of their help.
- Carol Ramelb, our typesetter and graphics artist, who also has a fine eye for text.
- Martha Laxson who prepared the index.

Applying the Basic Principles of Writing

1.1

Effective business writing requires much more than correct grammar, punctuation, and spelling. While these aspects are important, the best writing clearly and concisely communicates its message. When you receive a phone call from your reader asking what you meant, you have obviously not communicated clearly. If your reader is offended by what you have written, you have lost an opportunity to build a positive relationship. And if no one even bothers to read your writing, you have wasted your valuable time.

Writing is, for most of us, a very personal and painful task. But guidelines for good writing can make this difficult job much easier and faster. Meaningful and practical guidelines begin with a quick review of the basic principles of effective communication. Keeping these principles in mind will immediately make your writing more successful.

1.1

FOCUS ON YOUR READER

The key to successful writing is to focus on what the *reader* needs to hear—not on what *you* want to say. Knowing as much as possible about your audience will determine what you say, how you say it, and how you organize it.

Jot down the answers to these three reader-focused questions before you start to write.

1. Who is my reader?
2. What does my reader need to know?
3. What does my reader want to hear?

Knowing the answers to these questions can help you begin to focus your message with confidence.

When writing to more than one reader, draw a strong mental picture of the "typical" person in that group. Then, write to that one reader.

1.2

DEVELOP A "SERVICE" ATTITUDE

Think of every reader as a customer. It makes no difference whether your reader is the general public, an employee of another office, someone you work with, or even, if you are a student, your teacher. When you see the reader as your customer, you will want to provide this person with the best possible service and information. Use the following techniques to achieve this "service attitude."

1.2.1 Use "you" in your letters and memos

Look at samples of your own writing. If your letters and memos are peppered with "I" and "we," you are probably focusing your message on what *you* want to say rather than on what your *reader* needs to know.

One Warning About *You*

Don't appear as if you are accusing or blaming the reader.

Poor:	You failed to meet the deadline.
Better:	We received your bid after the May 1 deadline.
Poor:	You did not complete your job application form correctly.
Better:	Please complete line 4 of your job application, and sign on line 12.

1.2.1

> ### Avoid Negative Words
>
> How do you feel after reading the words on this list?
>
> | | |
> |---|---|
> | Dispute | Neglect |
> | Problem | Prohibit |
> | Regret | Reject |
> | Unfair | Worry |
>
> Depressed? This is how your readers feel when they read negative words. Use positive language.

Using "you" in your letters and memos will automatically force you to concentrate on what is important to the reader. Look at how this familiar-sounding sentence begins.

> I am pleased to inform you that you have been selected as the new coordinator of the Highlands Dam Project.

Does your reader care that you are pleased? Of course not! Try:

> Congratulations! You have been selected as the new coordinator of the Highlands Dam Project.

What is important to the reader in the next example?

> We have asked that a copy of the Helium Corporation's annual report be sent to you.

So what that you have asked! Most readers would like to know when they are going to receive the report. It is an easy matter to put "you" up front and refocus the sentence.

> You should receive your copy of *Lighten Up*, the Helium Corporation's annual report, by April 7.

1.2.2 Tell the reader what *can* be done, not what *can't*

Your reader will appreciate your message when you focus on the positive.

No: People who have not been employees for at least six months may not participate in the "Employee of the Year" program.

Yes: Anyone who has been employed for at least six months is eligible for the "Employee of the Year" program.

No: You are reminded that the law prohibits the construction of access roads without a permit granted by this department.

Yes: To construct the access road, you will need a permit from this department.

1.2.3 Help your reader

Show readers that you care by taking an extra step to help them.

No: We are not responsible for mosquito eradication. We suggest you try the Department of Health to see if someone there will help you.

Yes: I have contacted Bill Thompson at the Department of Health, Vector Control, who can help you. Please call him at 765-1234 to give him more specific information about the drainage in your area.

1.3

WRITE IN A NATURAL STYLE

Don't create a "paper monster" that makes you sound bureaucratic or legalistic. Make your writing readable by using a natural-sounding style.

1.3.1 Avoid pompous words and phrases

1.3.1

> Pursuant to the above referenced matter, a re-analysis of your expense report reflects a discrepancy in the manner in which it was computed.

Sometimes we think our letters sound more "businesslike" when we sprinkle them with inflated words and phrases as in the previous example. More often, these words and phrases do not make us look more important or "legal"; they only make us sound pompous. It would be easier on readers if you rewrote the opening sentence to say

> You are right. You did make only six trips out of town last month.

If you find a phrase going down onto the paper too quickly, check to see if it is one of those pompous clichés that litter business writing. Then, use a more natural-sounding phrase.

POMPOUS	NATURAL
Aforementioned	Previous
Ascertain	Determine
Assistance	Help
Attached herewith	Enclosed
Enclosed herewith	Enclosed
Facilitate	Help
Finalize	Complete; finish
Forthwith	At once
Hereafter; heretofore; hereby	(Eliminate)
Humbly request	Ask
I am cognizant of	I know

1.3.1

Jargon

When writing to people outside your area of expertise, don't use jargon or occupational "lingo."

No: Our department's multidimensional, multi-ethnic, and multifaceted program is designed to facilitate the individual's performance capability in interfacing with the community-at-large.

Yes: Our department's new training program will make it easier for you to work with our clients.

I am in receipt of	I have
Kindly advise	Let us know
Optimal	Best
Pending your reply	Until I hear from you
Per our conversation	When we spoke
Please be advised	(Eliminate)
Pursuant to	Concerning
Take under advisement	Consider
The undersigned/ the writer	I
Utilize; usage	Use
With reference to	Regarding; about
Your communication	Your call, your letter

1.3.3

> ### When Someone Else Is Signing
>
> When writing a letter for another person's signature, you may refer to your department as "we" and the actions you have taken as "departmental actions." However, be careful about including too many of these expressions.
>
> Generally, the person *signing* should be the one to personalize the letter by using "I" and "me."

1.3.2 Use "I" when referring to yourself

Don't make your writing impersonal by using the royal "we" or by calling attention to yourself with words like the "undersigned." Instead, use "I."

No: If we can be of further assistance, please call us at 548-1234, or write to our office.

Yes: Whenever I can be of help, please call me at 548-1234, or write to me at 310 Center Street, Caspian, AZ 85734.

No: The undersigned telephonically interviewed the subject on March 17.

Yes: I spoke with Mrs. Kinder by phone on March 17.

1.3.3 Use the active voice

Conversational writing is usually "active" writing. Being "active" means that there is a "doer" who "does" something.

Passive: It is felt that more accurate employee time clocks are necessary in the factory environment.

Active: The consultant said we should install more accurate time clocks in our factories.

A Special Note on "I" for Report Writers

In some of your reports, you will want to keep the reader's focus on your ideas and not on your personal relationship. As a result, you should avoid "I" (and "you") in this more formal writing and use "he," "she," "it," and "they." However, even though you are not "conversing" with your reader, the other reader-centered principles discussed in this chapter still apply.

Passive: Your acknowledgment of this letter by phone call to Sherrie Singleton is required.

Active: Please call Sherrie Singleton (768-1234) to let her know that you have received this letter. [*The "doer" here is the unwritten "you."*]

1.4

REDUCE WORDINESS

Make reading easy for the reader: use fewer words. A good guideline to remember is that the average sentence length should be about 17 to 22 words or two typed lines. If most of your sentences are exceeding the 22-word limit, you are probably being wordy. Break up your longer sentences or cut unnecessary words.

Remember, however, that good writing uses sentences of varying lengths.

1.4.1 Eliminate unnecessary words from each sentence

Take time after you write the first draft to get rid of empty words and phrases. Cutting two or three words

1.4.2

Sometimes the Passive Is Best

Use the passive voice when you do not know who committed the action or when you want to emphasize the receiver of the action.

The error was discovered yesterday. [*In this case, the writer does not know or does not want to state who discovered the error.*]

A grievance was filed against the department. [*Here, the writer wants to emphasize the grievance, not who filed it.*]

from each sentence or rewriting long sentences more concisely will shrink your "paper monster."

Wordy: As you know, we all have the problem of not having enough funds to do all of the things that we want to do or need to be done and must allot the limited funds to areas that we feel will bring the best results. (45 words)

Concise: We must work together to spend our limited funds wisely. (10 words)

1.4.2 Cut clichés and empty phrases

Many of the wordy and empty phrases that clutter your messages are holdovers from outdated writing. These clichés are passed from generation to generation, resulting in "gobbledygook." Because these phrases cloud your message, ruthlessly cut them from your writing.

AVOID THIS	USE THIS
arrived at the conclusion	concluded
at this point in time	now

because of the fact that	because
come to terms with	agree; accept
connect together	connect
during the month of May	during May
during the same time that	while
eight in number	eight
for the purpose of providing	to provide
has the capability of working	works
held a meeting	met
important essentials	essentials
in a great many instances	often
in an effort to	to
in order to	to
in the development of	in developing
in the event that	if
involving a great deal of expense	costly; expensive
long period of time	long time
make an investigation	investigate
on account of the fact that	because
prior to that time	before
put in an appearance	came
remember the fact that	remember
return back	return
shows a tendency to	tends
similar in character to	similar to; like

1.4.2

situated in the vicinity of	near
until such time as you can	until you can
was of the opinion that	believed

Organizing Your Letters and Memos

2

2.1.1

Quickly organize your letters and memos by concentrating on the reader. If the reader will view your message as good or neutral news, use the *direct approach*. This three-part formula gets right to the point by classifying the information in terms of its importance to the reader. For bad news or persuasive situations in which you expect resistance, use the *indirect approach*. This four-part formula emphasizes reasons over decisions. Always remember that the approach you take depends on what your reader wants to hear.

2.1

THE DIRECT APPROACH

About 80 percent of your writing will use the direct approach. This emphasizes the most important idea for the reader by placing it in the opening of the message. Next, it clearly explains that idea. Finally, it closes on a positive note.

1. Open with the most important idea.
2. Explain that idea.
3. Close on a positive, friendly note.

2.1.1 Part One: Open with the main idea

Think of the one idea that your reader needs to know and put that up front. Don't keep your reader guessing.

Variations of the following examples can be used when the *main point* of the letter or memo is to

1. Let the reader know that a proposal or recommendation has been accepted:

Don't "Beat Around the Bush"

1. In the good news opening, don't routinely thank your reader for writing to you.

   No: Thank you for your letter of June 22.

   Instead, use the close of your letter to thank the reader for showing concern or interest.

2. Don't waste valuable space by telling the reader that you have received a letter.

   No: I am in receipt of your letter of March 25.

   Obviously, you have received the letter, or you wouldn't be writing.

3. If you have a continuing correspondence with the reader, you can refer to a previous message with a subject line.

   Subject: October 28 request for information on garlic production

---

Your proposal for an in-house stress clinic has been approved by our Division Chief.

2. Respond to a request:

Here are the latest publications we have concerning our company's garlic holdings.

3. Confirm what was previously discussed:

This letter is to confirm our November 10 telephone conversation in which you agreed to accept Hot Pepper Company's offer of settlement.

A MEMO: DIRECT APPROACH

2.1.1

November 2, 19___

To: Ann Souza
           Economic Analyst
           Planning Department

From: Jack Armstrong
           Agricultural Specialist
           Research Division

Subject: October 28 request for
           materials on garlic produc-
           tion

To-the-Point Opening

Here are the latest publications
concerning our company's garlic
holdings.

Brief but Adequate Explanation of Enclosures. Taking That Extra Step

"Growing Garlic" focuses on the
methods our suppliers use to cultivate this useful plant. The other
report, "Garlic Economics," discusses the impact of garlic production
on the company's operations. You
might find pages five and six particularly relevant to your study.

Willingness to Be of Help and Positive Close

Please call me at 967-1234 should
you need additional information. I
wish you much success with your project.

Enclosures (2)

A LETTER: DIRECT APPROACH

April 7, 19__

Mr. George Able, President
Stress Clinic, Inc.
1272 Britannia Street
Stockton, CA 95798

Dear Mr. Able:

Your proposal for an in-house stress clinic has been approved by our Department Chief. We are very excited about getting started on this project.

Most Important Idea for the Reader

To receive the necessary federal funding for the project, please complete the enclosed "Contract Preparation" and "Federal Contractors Information" forms by May 1.

Explanation of First Detail with Motivation for Action

These completed forms should be sent to Ms. Martha Watson, Project Coordinator, City Mental Health Division, P.O. Box 207, Paris, IN 47456. Please call Ms. Watson at 548-1234 to arrange a meeting date to discuss further your project.

Explanation of Second Detail with All Relevant Information

All of us at the City Mental Health Division are looking forward to the clinic's contribution to a healthy environment.

Positive and Friendly Close

Yours truly,

Michael Mitchell
Special Projects Manager

MM:gp

Enclosures (2)

4. Thank the reader:

Your "Break Any Habit" luncheon speech was inspiring and effective. Thank you for motivating all of us to begin breaking unproductive work habits.

5. Ask for information:

Please answer the following questions about the training materials you advertised in your March issue of *New Training Age* magazine.

2.1.2 Part Two: Explain the idea

Once you have presented the main idea, explain it. If there is more than one point to discuss, present each in the order of importance for the reader.

EXAMPLE:

To receive the necessary federal funding for the project, please complete the enclosed "Contract Preparation" and "Federal Contractors Information" forms by May 1.

These completed forms should be sent to Ms. Martha Watson, Project Coordinator, City Mental Health Division, P.O. Box 207, Paris, IN 47456. Please call Ms. Watson at 548-1234 to arrange a meeting date to discuss further your project.

EXAMPLE:

"Growing Garlic" focuses on the methods our suppliers use to cultivate this useful plant. The other report, "Garlic Economics," discusses the impact of garlic production on the company's profits. You might find pages five and six of this publication particularly relevant to your study.

2.1.3 Part Three: Close on a positive note

Write a positive, friendly close to your letters and memos. When necessary, be sure to include the contact person and telephone number.

EXAMPLE:

All of us at the City Mental Health Division are looking forward to the clinic's contribution to a healthier environment.

EXAMPLE:

Please call me at 548-1234 should you need additional information. I wish you much success with your project.

2.2

2.2

THE INDIRECT APPROACH

No one likes to hear "No." This is why writing bad news calls for all your tact and public relations skills. In presenting negative news to the reader, be careful that you don't appear cold or bureaucratic. Show the reader that you really are concerned by using the four-part indirect approach. Begin with a neutral or positive statement; next, courteously explain the reasons for the decision; then, present the decision; finally, close on a friendly note.

1. Open with a neutral or positive statement.
2. Explain the circumstances.
3. Present the decision.
4. Close on a friendly note.

A MEMO: INDIRECT APPROACH

2.2

August 16, 19___

To: Lorrin Tanaka
         Supervisor, Landover Office

From: Travis Splain

Subject: Request for additional staff

Neutral Agreement

Your "short-handedness" is certainly creating a problem and I can appreciate what you are going through. With staff cutbacks and emergency leaves, my office is in much the same position as yours.

Lead-In to Explanation

Explanation of Relevant Reasons

During the period that you need extra help, we will be even more short-handed than usual. Three of our staff will be out: an unexpected surgery, an early pregnancy leave, and a long-planned trip to Japan.

Implied Denial and Counter-Proposal

I have discussed your situation with Lester Hayward at the Centerville office. He may have someone available for the time you requested. Please call Lester at 741-3338.

Willingness to Be of Help

Let me know if you need help after October 30; our office should have someone available then.

TS:mj

A LETTER: INDIRECT APPROACH

2.2

```
February 14, 19__

Mr. Royce Yount
621 Pauly Lane
Huntingdon, PA 16651

Dear Mr. Yount:

Your application for Ourbank's
CreditGuard Insurance has been
reviewed.

To qualify for this type of insur-
ance, the applicant must be under 65
years of age. Therefore, your appli-
cation cannot be processed.

Thank you for your interest in our
insurance program. Should you have
questions about any of Ourbank's
other services, please call me at
538-1134.

Sincerely,


Beatriz Loo
Senior Underwriting Representative
```

Neutral Opening

Objective Explanation and Decision

Positive Close

2.2.1 Part One: Open with a neutral statement

Jumping right in and announcing the bad news in the first sentence often stops the reader from going any further. A good strategy for bad news, then, is to begin with a neutral or positive statement that sets up a review of the facts.

Here are possible ways to begin the bad-news letter.

1. Give any good news you might have:

Your request for a fax machine has been approved. [*Later, you will refuse the reader's other request for additional office space.*]

2. Express agreement when possible:

Your "short-handedness" is certainly a problem and I can appreciate what you are going through. [*Later, you will refuse the reader's request for additional help.*]

3. Refer to the previous correspondence:

This letter is in response to your request for a contract extension.

4. Tell the reader the information has been given to you for reply:

Your letter and application for Ourbank's CreditGuard Insurance has been sent to me by the branch manager.

5. Outline any action that has been taken:

The Management Efficiency Committee met three days this week to discuss your case.

6. Express appreciation:

Thank you for giving us the opportunity to discuss the details which led to our decision.

Don't Express False Hope

No: I was very pleased to receive your letter asking me to speak at your meeting. [This sounds as if you are going to say "yes."]

Your opening should lead smoothly into the explanation. If you must follow it with "however," the opening should be rewritten.

Keep the opening short—no more than two or three lines.

2.2.2 Part Two: Explain the circumstances

Always present at least one good reason for the decision except in cases where the reasoning behind the decision must be kept confidential. The most persuasive reason shows that the decision is in the best interest of either the reader or a large group of people.

EXAMPLE:

To ensure the confidentiality of our employees, personnel files may be examined only with the employee's written permission.

With bad-news letters, it is especially important that the facts be presented in a neutral manner. Careful and clear explanations of policies and regulations will make the reader more inclined to listen to what you have to say.

EXAMPLE:

Our policy regulations for unsolicited proposals state that when people in an office need training, in-house resources must be checked first. If these resources are not available and the proposed training exceeds $4,000, then a contract is awarded only with the approval of our company's comptrollers.

2.2.3

Everyone Wants Respect

In bad-news letters, it is especially important that the tone of your message be friendly and courteous. Don't talk down to your reader.

No: To help you better understand your IRA, don't hesitate to call me.

And don't sound like you distrust the reader.

No: If, as you claim, you are unable to meet the deadline, we will consider an extension.

Instead, show a more respectful tone:

Yes: Whenever you have questions concerning your IRA, please call me at 321-7654.

Yes: Please let us know if you need an extension.

2.2.3 Part Three: Present the decision

If the reason or explanation is strong enough, you don't have to say "no" explicitly.

I will be in New York on the day you would like me to speak. [*The reason is clear; you do not have to add, "Therefore, I will be unable to attend."*]

But if a decision must be stated, there are two effective ways to do so.

1. Offer a compromise or counterproposal:

I have discussed your situation with Lester Hayward at the Homedale facility. He may have someone available for the time you requested.

2. State the bad news or negative decision firmly and clearly, but do so just once:

Therefore, your application cannot be processed.

The Apology

Don't apologize for bad news if you have given a good reason. Such apologies sound empty.

We are sorry we are returning your application.

If you really were sorry, you wouldn't return the application.

Moreover, an apology is often interpreted as an acceptance of liability even though no such acceptance is intended. If you must apologize in your writing, apologize for *inconvenience* or *disappointment*—and state it only once.

2.2.4 Part Four: Close on a friendly note

Write a brief, friendly close which looks forward to future communication.

Here are some possible ways of closing the bad-news letter.

1. If you have offered a counterproposal or compromise, state what the reader should do:

When you have decided which option you want, please call me at 735-4739.

2. Express appreciation for the reader's interest:

Thank you for sharing your training proposal with us.

3. Ask if there are any questions:

Should you have any questions, please call me at 548-1234.

> ### "Please Feel Free . . ."
>
> Don't write, "Please feel free to call" or "Please do not hesitate to call." In the first example, you are giving permission. In the second example, no one should ever feel hesitant about calling you.

2.3

THE DIRECT MESSAGE FORMAT

1. Open with the most important idea:
   - (a) Present best news; or
   - (b) Present main idea/s.

2. Explain by using one or more of the following:
   - (a) Include all necessary details;
   - (b) Provide educational information;
   - (c) Suggest other services or ideas.

3. Close on a positive note:
   - (a) Be positive, friendly;
   - (b) If necessary, state desired reader action;
   - (c) If appropriate, show appreciation and willingness to be of further assistance;
   - (d) When there is nothing to say, just stop.

2.4

THE INDIRECT MESSAGE FORMAT

1. Open with a buffer:
   (a) Share good news;
   (b) Express appreciation;
   (c) Show agreement.
2. Explain the circumstances, unless confidential:
   (a) Show action is in reader's best interest;
   (b) Explain courteously all pertinent facts behind decision.
3. Present the decision using one of the following:
   (a) When reason is very strong, allow reader to conclude that response is negative. Do not reiterate bad news.
   (b) Offer constructive suggestion, counterproposal, or alternative course of action.
   (c) Express decision briefly and as positively as possible.
4. Close on a friendly note:
   (a) State necessary future action if counterproposal was offered;
   (b) Show appreciation;
   (c) Be positive and friendly;
   (d) Express continued interest and reader benefit;
   (e) Invite future patronage.

Writing Effective Reports

All the considerations discussed so far for letters and memos apply to the report writing process as well. This process is more complex, however, because it usually involves research and the product is generally longer. Because of this complexity, use this nine-step process in organizing your report writing:

1. Understand the assignment.
2. Gather the data.
3. Analyze the data.
4. Determine the main point.
5. Outline the report.
6. Write the report.
7. Consider graphics.
8. Format the report.
9. Edit carefully.

Following this process allows you to organize your work in a systematic way. It also helps you allocate more accurately the time needed for the project. Finally, as a systematic writer, you will rarely have writer's block because completing one step successfully leads you naturally into the next step.

Using the Process

Use the process to pinpoint trouble spots. If you can't complete a step, go to the preceding step; the problem usually lies there. For example, if you can't outline, it is usually because you haven't a clear main point; or if you can't state a main point, it is generally because you haven't analyzed the data thoroughly.

3.1

UNDERSTAND THE ASSIGNMENT

Rushing off to the word processor as soon as you are told to write a report is an enthusiastic but often fruitless way to begin. Before you start, take time to consider the essential questions which form all reports.

3.1.1 Consider how the report will be used

As with any writing project, begin with the three reader-centered questions mentioned in Chapter 1:

1. Who is my reader?
2. What does my reader need to know?
3. What does my reader want to hear?

Then, for report writing, add a fourth question:

4. How will my reader use this material?

Answering this last question should help you know what material to gather and how to organize and format the report.

3.1.2 Know what the person who requested the report expects from it

Very few people write reports for the fun of it. Most are told to write. Because this is the case, it is always a good idea to discuss with the person who has asked you to write the report (the "authorizer" in business jargon) exactly what is expected. Ask as many questions as you must to clarify what you are supposed to do. Remember, it is better to appear "lost" or "confused" at the beginning and be able to turn in a report that the authorizer wants than to look "smart" and find out that your report is not at all what was expected.

3.1.2

A good technique to use—especially when you are not certain that you understand precisely what is expected—is to state your assignment as specifically as possible in writing. Use either a question or an infinitive phrase.

Question:

What is the feasibility of planting Japanese cherry trees in front of our Central Avenue building and parking lot?

Infinitive:

To determine the feasibility of planting Japanese cherry trees along the Central Avenue building and parking lot

Question:

What has caused the recent rise in attrition at our home office?

Infinitive:

To determine the causes for the recent rise in attrition at our home office

Collaborate with the Authorizer

Sometimes you will discover that the person who has asked you to write doesn't have a very clear idea of what the report should contain. This is a time to collaborate with the authorizer. Discuss the project thoroughly before beginning; then meet, discuss, and agree on each step of the writing process before moving on to the next. While this conferencing will take initial effort, it will save much time and grief later because the report will contain the focus both of you want.

3.2

GATHER THE DATA

Once you know what kind of research is expected, gather the data.

3.2.1 List the factors

Begin by making a list of the factors that your report must contain to be complete.

Assignment:

To determine the feasibility of planting Japanese cherry trees in front of our Central Avenue building and parking lot

Factors to Be Considered:
1. Soil conditions along Central Avenue
2. Type of cherry blossom tree
3. Traffic conditions
4. Type of equipment necessary

3.2.2 List appropriate data and resources

Add to each factor the types of data that may be useful, and note where you will find them. Finish this step by gathering and reviewing those resources systematically.

Factors and Data to Be Considered:

1. *Soil conditions along Central Avenue*
   Soil composition
   Drainage
   Acidity
   (Have soil sample analyzed at State Department of Agriculture)

2. *Type of cherry blossom tree*
Possible species and costs
Growth conditions of each species
Appearance of each species
(Review literature listed in the on-line catalog at the
university's Botany Department. Call Kent Billingsworth
at Cloverdale Nursery concerning availability of stock.)

3. *Traffic conditions*
Effect of exhaust fumes or other pollution on plants
Possible interference with traffic signs or stop lights in
area
(Check with city's Department of Transportation.)

4. *Type of equipment necessary*
Planting—Post hole digger, plow, other equipment,
cost?
Maintenance—Sprinkler system, fertilizer, other, cost?
(Ask Facilities Department about availability.)

Four types of data are commonly available to you.
Each has advantages and disadvantages.

In-House Data. Data, gathered from the workplace,
such as reports, letters, memos, and account sheets, is
probably the most specific and relevant information
available for an in-house report. Keep in mind, however, that in-house data may provide biased information
and can be prejudiced by management opinions and
attitudes.

Is It "Data Is" or "Data Are"?

Have you ever wondered why some people use
data with a singular verb ("data is") and others
insist that it should be used with a plural verb
("data are")? See *data* in Chapter 7, "Using Words
Correctly," for the answer.

3.2.2

Library Materials or Databases. These materials often provide excellent background information and, in terms of most projects, are considered the most objective. However, because they are not specific to your assignment, the relevance of this information to your report must be explained clearly to the reader.

Observed and Experiential Data. The easiest information to gather, this type of data can add specific insight to your report. Experiential data is usually, however, based on feelings and has to be carefully considered before being used.

Surveys. Surveys are excellent ways of discovering how people feel about a given subject. Often, they are used to predict how people might act in a certain situation. As such, they can be useful sources for you. Surveys are not, however, truth; they only tabulate responses. Just because a survey indicates that most of those surveyed find the air clean enough, it doesn't mean that the air *is* clean.

"Let's Do a Survey!"

Often, particularly when you are working in a group, somebody will suggest that you should quickly run out and conduct a survey. Accurate surveying is a scientific and arduous task involving a great deal of trial-and-effort refinement before reaching an acceptable level of accuracy. Before you get trapped by the fascinating attraction of a survey, consider carefully whether you have the time, expertise, need, and energy to conduct one.

3.3

ANALYZE THE DATA

Analyzing the data you have gathered generally involves two tasks: reviewing it for the common communication problems and drawing logical assertions.

3.3.1 Check for common communication problems

Your data can have these three most common communication errors: subjective viewpoint, imprecise language, and physical limitations.

Subjective Viewpoint. Most people are prone to letting feelings dictate and interpret facts. If we like something, we generally find positive examples to describe it; if we dislike something, we find negative examples. Try to determine if you or your source is letting feelings dictate what is being described.

Imprecise Language. Similar to the subjective viewpoint is imprecise language. The most common form of imprecise language is the use of *abstractions* or general words to describe a multitude of specific actions. For example, we may describe a car as going fast. But, depending on the situation, "fast," an abstraction, could be 10, 20, 60, or 100 miles an hour. Unless the reader knows precisely what "fast" means and the context in which it is being used, confusion is likely.

Physical Limitations. Police officers find that witnesses will give very complete and precise descriptions of what they have "seen" even though these witnesses couldn't have really seen the entire accident. These people are filling in the information gaps with plausible solutions. Sometimes the solutions are so probable that the witness imagines having seen each step of the process. As a writer, you can make major errors if you don't determine early on whether the information you are using is based on a complete first-hand account or was fabricated from bits and pieces and then rendered whole by the imagination.

3.3.2 Make logical assertions

Once the data has been analyzed, you will begin to make assertions. Assertions will become the main points of your report. The credibility of your assertions is based on the quality of your evidence and the logical relationship between your evidence and assertions.

Assume, for example, in your research, you have discovered the following facts:

Japanese cherry trees grow only in volcanic soil.

The soil in front of your Central Avenue building is 80 percent lime based.

You would then be able to make the following assertion.

The soil in front of your Central Avenue building is not conducive to growing Japanese cherry trees.

This would be logical.

Keep Your Credibility

To avoid losing credibility because of a logical error, check each of your assertions carefully to ensure that you haven't left out information or haven't let a particular perspective blind you to possibilities. The careful report writer will also become an imaginary hostile audience and try to disprove each assertion before using it.

3.4

DETERMINE THE MAIN POINT

The next step is to gather all the assertions and add them up. The total is the main point you will make in your report.

Main Point:

Given present conditions, Japanese cherry trees will not grow successfully in front of the Central Avenue building.

Assertion:

The soil is not conducive to growing cherry trees.

Assertion:

The amount of exhaust from passing traffic is potentially "dangerous" to Japanese cherry trees.

Assertion:

The sewage and electrical systems under the ground will interfere with the root growth.

Main Point:

An examination of recent employee exit interviews indicates three important reasons for increased attrition rates at C & R Manufacturing.

Assertion:

The company moved its main plant to the opposite side of the city.

Assertion:

Company benefits decreased by 30 percent.

Assertion:

Management reorganization reduced the number of senior level positions by one-third.

Put it in Writing

Lee Iaccoca, the former head of Chrysler Motor Co., said it well:

". . . the discipline of writing something down is the first step toward making it happen. . . . There is something about putting your thoughts on paper that forces you to get down to specifics."

Specifically, put this into effect by writing out the main idea and posting it near your workspace. If you are working with a word processor or word processing software, type the main idea at the beginning of the file. Review it each time you work on the report. It will become the most important guideline you could have.

3.5

OUTLINE THE REPORT

You will be a more efficient writer if you outline thoughts before committing them to paper. This saves time by forcing you to think the problem through before writing.

When you outline, keep your reader's point of view in mind. Using your reader as a guide, determine the overall approach and the most effective ordering of your ideas.

3.5.1 Determine the overall approach

If the main idea is good or neutral news for the reader, the direct approach discussed in Chapter 2 will work. If the reader won't like the information or will need to be persuaded, use the indirect approach (also discussed in Chapter 2).

3.5.2

In the example concerning attrition, if the personnel manager of the company has asked you to summarize the company's exit interviews and your report does not reflect negatively on the personnel manager, use the direct approach. The main point, therefore, will be placed in the first part or introduction of the report.

On the other hand, if the president of the company has just returned from springtime in Washington, D.C. and has her heart set on a blossoming cherry tree screen for the Central Avenue building, the indirect method might be a better choice. Then, the main point would come at the end of the report. In this case, it also might be politically wise to suggest other options to the reader.

Can There Be a Neutral "No"?

Just because you are going to say "no" does not necessarily mean that the report should use the indirect method. If the reader only wants information or has no stake in your answer, the direct method should be used.

3.5.2 Determine the order of the assertions

How the assertions are ordered within the report will depend on the purpose of the report and the natural flow of the content. Generally, there are three patterns: the chronological, the spatial, and the topical patterns.

The *chronological pattern* places the report's points in time order. Use this pattern for reports that emphasize the history of a problem or idea.

Main Point:

A correlation can be drawn between three recent management decisions and increased attrition rates at the home office of C & R Manufacturing.

1. The first wave of resignations occurred in January after the company moved its main building to the opposite side of the city.

2. A second wave occurred in March when company benefits decreased by 30 percent.

3. The third wave occurred when the recent management reorganization reduced the number of senior level positions by one-third.

The *spatial* or *descriptive pattern* organizes the information in terms of how an object or area appears in space. Technical writers and engineers use the spatial pattern to describe physical projects. Many other things, from the structure of a company to the layout of a computer circuit, can also be developed spatially.

Main Point:

Given present conditions, Japanese cherry trees will not grow successfully in front of the Central Avenue building.

1. The top soil next to the building is not conducive to growing cherry trees.

2. The substrata below the top soil will not allow for the drainage necessary for Japanese cherry trees.

3. Below the substrata, there is an underlying network of sewage and electrical piping that will not allow the trees to develop essential root growth.

The *topical pattern* is the most common because it is the most flexible. Any number of thinking patterns—reasons, cause and effect, problem/solution, order of importance, or order of persuasiveness, for example—can be used.

Main Point:

An examination of recent employee exit interviews indicates three important reasons for increased attrition rates at C & R Manufacturing.

1. The company moved its main plant to the opposite side of the city.

2. Company benefits decreased by 30 percent.

3. Management reorganization reduced the number of senior level positions by one-third.

3.6

WRITE THE REPORT

Only after you have completed all the previous steps should you sit down to write. There are three helpful techniques for report writers to keep in mind as they draft the report.

3.6.1 Draft quickly

Set aside time to write and draft quickly. Try to keep the ideas expressed in Chapter 1 in mind as you write, but don't waste time agonizing over the grammar or style. Save that agony for the editing step.

An Interesting Fact

The average working person is interrupted at least once every two and a half minutes. This does not allow you a great deal of time to work out a concentrated flow in the writing. In fact, if you don't write quickly, there is a good chance that you will forget the main thrust of your writing.

3.6.2 Write from the middle

If you are like most people, the first few paragraphs are the hardest to compose. You aren't sure what approach to take or how to elicit the reader's interest. This problem can be overcome easily by starting at the middle of the document.

Use your outline as a guide, and begin writing the report from the body. Once the body is completed, draft the conclusion. By the time you have finished the conclusion, you should have the essential idea for the introduction.

Don't Assume

Don't assume the reader will make the same creative jumps you have. While working on your report, try to explain even the most complex ideas as if you were explaining them to someone who knows little about your project.

3.6.3 Use the paragraph as the unit of composition

There are three types of paragraphs used in report writing: body, concluding, and introductory paragraphs. Use these as the units of composition.

Body Paragraphs. Body paragraphs show the development of your ideas. They are easier for the reader to follow when they begin with a topic sentence that is followed by several sentences of specific explanation or example. In developing the body paragraphs, present ideas in predetermined thinking patterns. The following are among the most common:

Time:

Topic Sentence	**Over the last 30 years, the number of women in the U.S. labor force has steadily increased.** In fact, since the end of World War II, women have accounted for about 60 percent of the net growth of
Decade #1	the labor force. In 1950, according to the Bureau of Labor Statistics, slightly less than 35 percent of all women were employed
Decade #2	outside the home. By 1960, that number
Decade #3	was approximately 40 percent. In 1970, the percentage of women had increased to 45.
Decade #4	And by 1980, one woman out of two, or 50 percent, was part of the labor force. It is estimated that by the year 2000, as many as 80 percent of all women will be working.

Spatial:

3.6.3

Topic Sentence | **The keyboard, 16 by 5 inches, is slightly smaller than a standard keyboard.**
Top | Primarily this is because it is missing function keys across the top. Instead, the left
Left | hand space comprises a familiar "QWERTY" typewriter-like keyboard. On the right, the
Right | numbered keys are set up in a calculator formation.

Listing:

Topic Sentence | **Our committee has considered several factors in preparing our recommendation to schedule fact-finding field trips**
Point #1 | **to flood disaster areas.** First, trips will be arranged at places where meeting facilities are available and accessible to the public.
Point #2 | Also, to minimize disruption to the members' workdays, trips will be scheduled
Point #3 | either from 8 to 11 or from 12 to 3. Finally, although our committee feels strongly that these field trips are vital in providing a "hands-on" view of electrical damage in flood areas, the time spent on these trips must not keep us from completing the other critical tasks of the committee.

Problem/Solution:

Topic Sentence | **We would like to propose a new approach to the problem of absen-**
Problem | **teeism in our department.** Absences have increased 12 percent over the last six months. In addition, improvements we made to the working environment two months ago seem to have had no effect on

3.6.3

Solution

the problem. We are now considering using the "competitive teams" incentive program that has worked very well in other establishments. If this program is put into effect, we feel that absenteeism can be reduced by 90 percent.

Cause/Effect:

Topic Sentence

Cause

Effects

The incorrect installation of the Video Display Terminals (VDT) has resulted in poor employee performance. The terminals, which were put in a month ago, were placed in the wrong lighting conditions, at the wrong angle, and too low. As a result, our employees have experienced a number of problems. They have complained of an annoying glare from the reflection of room lighting on the screen. Besides experiencing eyestrain, employees have had low backaches because they have had to slump in their chairs to focus on the screens that were not placed high enough on the desks. Consequently, employee efficiency dropped 15 to 20 percent during the last month.

Concluding Paragraphs. Concluding paragraphs serve two functions: they summarize and they spell out the action the writer expects of the reader. Sometimes that action might simply be a nod of agreement, but just as often the report's conclusion will give a clear recommendation for action.

EXAMPLE:

Summary

Action

This research clearly indicates that SELECTO employees feel overworked, underpaid, and under-appreciated. To remedy this situation, the committee feels that the following recommendations should be instituted at once:

1. A 10-percent increase in salary for all personnel

2. A 25-percent increase in cost-of-living-allowances

3. A 20-percent increase in hiring over the next three years.

4. The establishment of personnel centers where employees can go to relax during a stressful day.

Introductory Paragraphs. Write the introduction last. Introductory paragraphs might refer to the authorization, include definitions, explain methods, or define scope. The introduction *must* clearly state the subject and the purpose of the report.

EXAMPLE:

Subject

Authorization

During May, a series of articles appearing in local newspapers reported that the salaries and self-esteem of utility company employees in the state were very low. As a result of these publications, the Chief Executive Officer's office asked on June 3 that our division investigate and report on employee self-esteem and attitude toward salaries. We were then asked to compare this data with data from other utility companies in the nation.

Definitions

For the purposes of this report, a "SELECTO Employee" is defined as any person employed on a full-time and regular basis by Selanese Electric Company. Positions expressly excluded are full-time employees on temporary contract or subcontract with SELECTO and employees of any SELECTO subsidiary.

Methods and Scope

The study included an examination of all salary records of SELECTO personnel hired over the last 10 years. Investigators for this study also conducted a survey of employees and compared the results with samples gathered at Oakland, California, and Alexandria, Virginia. This report will present the results of this data gathering, analyze those findings, and draw conclusions from the data.

Purpose

Use the Beginning and the End

The average reader will read the beginning of the report to find out what it is about and flip to the end to find out if and when action might be required. Take advantage of this reading habit and ensure that the important ideas of your report are placed in either of these places where the reader will most likely find them.

3.7

CONSIDER GRAPHICS

3.8

Review your draft to see if there are any sections of numerical detail that could be made clearer with a chart or a graph. Spatial details can also be made easier for the reader when you include a drawing or a picture. Remember, however, your report should not rely entirely on these visual aids.

It is also important to refer to the graphic with an introductory sentence such as: "Figure 1 is an example of the employee evaluation form." A sentence or two of interpretation might then follow the introductory sentence. (A discussion of formatting graphics is located in Chapter 8.)

"See Attached Drawing"

Avoid the temptation to treat a graphic as self-explanatory—it rarely is. Make sure you use your best sense of spatial organization to describe the graphic to the reader and to highlight the important information.

3.8

FORMAT THE REPORT

The purpose of the formatting is not to show off your computer's capabilities but to visualize your ideas for the reader. As such, formatting is an essential task for the careful report writer. In general, there are several formatting points to consider. (Chapter 8 contains more information about placing graphics and formatting the report.)

3.8.1 Use headings to emphasize your ideas

3.8.3

The best headings are "talking captions" that speak to the reader. Avoid headings in the body which simply lay out the parts of the report. They are essentially useless for the reader.

> **No:** Body
> A. Point One
> B. Point Two
> C. Point Three

> **Yes:** SECURITY AT RASCALS, INC.
> A. Necessary Elements of a Security System
> B. Standards for Judging Security Effectiveness
> C. Alternative Plan for Security Improvement

3.8.2 Use empty space to lighten the reader's load

A dense page of text makes for dread in the hearts of most readers. Lighten your text by using as much white space as possible. Also, use double spacing and headings to break up the text.

3.8.3 Use shorter paragraphs to lighten the page

Try to ensure that every double-spaced page has at least two paragraphs and every single-spaced page at least four. If you are single spacing, double space between paragraphs. If a paragraph is much more than 250 words, find an appropriate place and divide it.

3.9

EDIT CAREFULLY

Read the text as many times as necessary to correct any errors in content and mechanics. As we suggest in Chapter 9, at one point you ought to read through the text at least three times: once to correct any errors in content and organization; once to correct grammar, spelling, and punctuation errors; and once to review for formatting consistency. Remember that the slightest error can sometimes mar the credibility of your report.

A SAMPLE SHORT REPORT: THE DIRECT APPROACH

3.9

To: James Dukes, Director
       Engineering Department

From: Jeanette Kim, Manager

RE: REMODELING PLANS

In our October staff meeting, you
mentioned that each department
should give input on Bowles Inc.'s
building remodeling plans. Our
staff would like to offer the following suggestions concerning our
office building in Moretown. The
ideas presented here have been
developed by our employee design
committee following a survey of
our employees. We feel these
changes will make our building a
showplace truly worthy of the
Auditing Department.

SOUTH END OF BUILDING: The cement
wall which runs across the south
end of the building should remain
as is. The view from this side of
the building is basically uninter-
esting, consisting of a warehouse
and a generator plant.

EAST END OF BUILDING: We do feel,
however, that the wall at the east
end of the building should be torn
down and that the parking lot be
made a landscape of wisteria and
oleander. This garden area can
then become a Moretown showplace.

Authorization
Subject
Purpose
Method
Main Point
Point #1
Point #2

A SAMPLE SHORT REPORT: THE DIRECT
APPROACH (continued)

3.9

NORTH WALL OF BUILDING: The north wall should also be razed and an addition constructed to include a marble terrace, swimming pool, sauna, hot tub, and employee lunch room.

Point #3

WEST WALL OF BUILDING: Finally, to smarten up the auditing offices, we would like to widen the west side of the building and move the garage. The general consensus is that a Hawaiian motif with rattan, ceiling fans, and Boston and asparagus ferns would be ideal. As you will see in Appendix 1, several local interior decorators have been suggested by the staff.

Point #4

We are presently working on plans to accommodate the computer terminals and the parking lot. Suggestions for these are included in Appendix 2.

Point #5

These, then, are the key ideas of our design plan. We would like to discuss them with the Facilities Board sometime next week. I will call you on Monday.

Summary Action

A. SAMPLE REPORT: THE INDIRECT APPROACH

3.9

June 4, 19___

TO: Marion J. Winklewoman
           Executive Assistant

FROM: Millard T. Dumforth
           Building Manager

SUBJECT: Japanese Cherry Trees on
           Central Avenue

This report is in response to Ms. Barchester's request two weeks ago for a feasibility study concerning planting "Japanese" or "Sato" Cherries along the Central Avenue side of our building.

Most of the people with whom I spoke were intrigued by the idea and agreed that, particularly in late spring and late autumn, the planting would be a spectacular addition to the city. Three factors were mentioned by all my sources regarding the successful planting of these trees.

1. Soil Conditions

According to Dr. Murray Quiverful of the Merkletown University Botany Department, Sato Cherries are very demanding of the soil. Such soil should be about 80 percent lime based. A soil sample analyzed by the University indicates that the soil along Central Avenue is predominantly volcanic—a direct opposite of the requirements for the Japanese cherry trees.

The soil, however, could be changed and periodically renourished to ensure successful propagation. Several sites in the

A SAMPLE REPORT: THE INDIRECT APPROACH (continued)

city already use this method for other plantings, though for smaller areas than our 1,200 foot strip.

2. Exhaust Fumes

Tests conducted by the City's Department of Transportation indicate that carbon dioxide (CO_2) exhaust emissions along the Central Avenue corridor are about 25 percent per cubic foot of oxygen. This means, according to Dr. Quiverful and most of the research on the subject, even if we succeed in getting the cherry trees to grow, the blooms would normally be brown, not pink, because of CO_2 poisoning.

We can, however, coat the trees with a liquid glass product that would allow the leaves to grow in a sort of individual protective greenhouse. Once again, other sites in the city have used this technique but on far fewer plants than the 60 we envision.

3. Underground Construction

Finally, the City Department of Public Works, to which I was referred by the Department of Transportation, mentioned that the sewage and electrical systems under the street are particularly shallow. As a result, there would have to be special accommodations to protect these utility structures. Figure 1 depicts the type of shield necessary.

A SAMPLE REPORT: THE INDIRECT
APPROACH (continued)

Figure 1

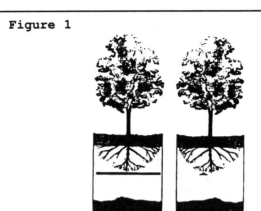

PROTECTIVE ROOT SHIELD
a. lengthwise; b. cross-section

Costs

The costs for these enhancements are out-
lined as follows:

```
COST OF PLANTS, INSTALLED
    60 trees @ $45.00 ea.      $    2,700
COST OF SOIL CHANGE
    1,200 feet @$500 per foot  $  600,000
LIQUID CLASS COATING
    60 trees @ $40 per tree     $    2,400
PROTECTIVE ROOT SHIELD
    1,200 feet @ $350 per foot $  420,000
SPRINKLER SYSTEM               $    2,400
    TOTAL                      $1,027,500
```

A SAMPLE REPORT: THE INDIRECT
APPROACH (continued)

A Cost-Effective Alternative

Because of the cost involved in planting
Sato Cherries, I also looked into an
alternative suggested by several of my
sources. This is *Cornus Florida* or the
Flowering Dogwood. Like the Sato Cherry,
the Flowering Dogwood blooms in midspring
and presents a spectacular display of
bloom heavy branches. Also, like the Sato
Cherry in autumn, the dogwood's foliage
turns a spectacular deep (wine) red before
the leaves fall.

Unlike the Sato Cherry, the flowering
Dogwood is a hardy plant that grows in
most soil conditions. Moreover, the blooms
are not affected by CO_2 and the root system is shallow. Lastly, the plants are
easily replaced should any need to be
removed for underground work.

```
COST OF PLANTS, INSTALLED
   60 trees @ $45.00 ea.     $2,700
SPRINKLER SYSTEM             $2,400
   TOTAL                     $5,100
```

Appendix
"Japanese" Cherry Trees

The "Japanese" cherry is the result of
over 300 years of crossbreeding and selec-
tive grafting. While there are no records
of the actual species involved in the
development of this group of ornamental
trees, Japanese records report their exis-
tence throughout the country from the sev-
enteenth century onward. Older botany

A SAMPLE REPORT: THE INDIRECT APPROACH (continued)

3.9

guides refer to them as *Prunus serralata*, var. *spontanea*, but in recent years the trees have been grouped under the Japanese name, "Sato" or "domestic" cherries.

While Sato Cherries are now relatively scarce in the United States, they were very popular in this country around the turn of the century, particularly after the Mayor of Tokyo gifted Washington, D.C. with its famous stand in 1911. Presently, there are scattered plantings on the east and the Pacific Northwest coasts of the North American continent.

The trees are deciduous, standing as high as 30 feet. The pointed leaves, as much as eight inches long, are green in the early spring through late fall when they turn a wine red before falling. In the late spring (late April and early May) the leaves are hidden by an abundance of pink or white blossoms. The trees are propagated by grafting.

3.10

THE REPORT WRITING PROCESS

1. Understand the assignment.
2. Gather the data for the report.
3. Analyze the data:
   (a) Recognize the common communication errors;
   (b) Distinguish facts, inferences, and opinions.
4. Review assertions for logic.
5. Draw an overall conclusion.
6. Organize and outline the report.
   (a) Determine the organizational approach.
   (b) Write a clear purpose statement.
   (c) Outline the body:
      I. Narrative organization;
      II. Descriptive organization;
      III. Classification organization.
   (d) Develop the opening and closing.
7. Write the report:
   (a) Use natural, conversational style.
   (b) Avoid "big" words when "little" ones will do.
   (c) Use specific and concrete language.
   (d) Keep sentences to an average length of 17 to 22 words.
8. Develop appropriate graphics.
9. Format the report.
10. Edit the report.

Correcting Grammar

When readers notice grammatical errors, they become more concerned with the correctness of your writing than with the quality of your ideas. When this happens, your writing does not accomplish its purpose.

If you feel secure in your knowledge of grammar, carefully proofread your own work. If you don't feel secure about grammatical rules, ask another person who writes well to proofread your work. Above all, learn to recognize and correct the following grammatical problems.

4.1

SENTENCE FRAGMENTS

A sentence fragment is an incomplete sentence. There are two ways to correct this problem.

4.1.1 Join the fragment to the sentence that goes either immediately in front of it or immediately after it

No: He is an understanding person. Like my father.
["*Like my father*" is a fragment.]

Yes: He is an understanding person like my father.

No: Because eating always puts me in a good mood. She suggested eating a bowl of mango ice cream.
[*"Because eating always puts me in a good mood"* is a fragment.]

Yes: Because eating always puts me in a good mood, she suggested eating a bowl of mango ice cream.
[Sentences can begin with *"because"* if you want to emphasize the cause.]

4.1.2 Rewrite the sentence so that it expresses a complete thought

No: Having jogged through the park during my lunch hour.

Yes: Having jogged through the park during my lunch hour, I missed my surprise birthday party.

4.2

RUN-ON SENTENCES AND COMMA SPLICES

A run-on sentence is two or more sentences joined without punctuation.

The staff marched in the Fourth of July parade the company president rode in the red convertible.

A comma splice is two or more sentences joined by a comma.

The staff marched in the Fourth of July parade, the company president rode in the red convertible.

There are three ways to correct these errors.

4.2.1 Insert a period to separate the two sentences

Yes: The staff marched in the Fourth of July parade. The company president rode in the red convertible.

4.2.2 Use a semicolon to join two closely related sentences

Yes: The staff marched in the Fourth of July parade; the company president rode in the red convertible.

4.3.2

4.2.3 Use a conjunction to join the two sentences

> **Yes:** The staff marched in the Fourth of July parade, *but* the company president rode in the red convertible.

> **Yes:** *While* the staff marched in the Fourth of July parade, the company president rode in the red convertible.

4.3

SUBJECT/VERB DISAGREEMENT

A subject/verb disagreement occurs when the verb does not agree in number (singular or plural) with the subject. Remember the rules of subject/verb agreement.

4.3.1 A singular subject takes a singular verb

> **No:** *Everyone* in the offices *are* going to "The Big Camp Out" this weekend. [*"Everyone"* is singular; *"are"* is plural.]

> **Yes:** *Everyone* in the offices *is* going to "the Big Camp Out" this weekend.

4.3.2 A plural subject must have a plural verb

> **No:** The *names* for each position *has* been announced. [Don't be misled by the words between the subject and the verb, *"for each position."* *"Names"* is plural and *"has"* is singular.]

Yes: The *names* for each position *have* been announced.

Yes: *Nicholas and Kimberly are* going to represent the company.

4.3.3 In "either/or" and "neither/nor" constructions, the verb should agree with the subject closer to it

No: Either the secretary or the *engineer are* mistaken about when the report was completed.

Yes: Either the secretary or the *engineer is* mistaken about when the report was completed.

Yes: Either the secretary or the *engineers are* mistaken about when the report was completed.

Yes: *Are* either the *secretaries* or the engineer mistaken about when the report was completed?

4.4

UNCLEAR OR SHIFTING PRONOUN REFERENCE

A pronoun reference shift occurs when the writer uses pronouns inconsistently. There are two rules for correcting such shifts.

4.4.1 The pronoun should agree in number (either singular or plural) with the noun or pronoun to which it refers

No: *Each* of them said *they* were going to spend the weekend fishing in the mountains. [*"Each"* is singular; *"they"* is plural.]

4.4.1

Some Confusing Words as Subjects

A. Some pronouns that are always singular include the following:

anyone	either	no one
each	everyone	someone

B. Some pronouns such as "all" and "some" may be singular or plural depending on the writer's intent.

All is well. [*"All"* is seen as a unit.] *All were* at the dinner. [*"All"* is seen as separate people.]

He reviewed the proposals at the end of the week. *Some were* still incomplete. [*"Some"* refers to the separate proposals.]

We bought fifteen pounds of sugar for the fudge. *Some was* left over. [*"Some"* is seen as a unit.]

C. Collective nouns are singular when they refer to the group and plural when they refer to parts of the group. The following are some common collective nouns.

audience	couple	jury
class	crowd	staff
committee	family	troop

The *staff was* represented by Joe Chun. [*"Staff"* refers to the group.]

The *staff were* presenting their reports while the building was being evacuated. [*"Staff"* refers to the individual members.]

Yes: *Each* of them said *he* [if all men] was going to spend the weekend fishing in the mountains.

Yes: *Each* of them said *she* [if all women] was going to spend the weekend fishing in the mountains.

Yes: *All* of them said *they* were going to spend the weekend fishing in the mountains.

No: When you sign all *three copies* of the contract, please return *it* to my office.

Yes: When you sign all *three copies* of the contract, please return *them* to my office.

4.4.2 Consistently use the same pronoun to agree with the noun to which it refers

No: In completing these personnel forms, *one* should follow the directions carefully. Otherwise, *you* may have to wait an extra month for your paycheck.

Yes: In completing these forms, follow the directions carefully. [The subject *"you"* is implied.] Otherwise, *you* may have to wait an extra month for your paycheck.

4.5

FAULTY PARALLELISM

Faulty parallelism occurs when the writer uses different grammatical forms for ideas in a list or for two items connected by a conjunction.

4.5

Begin each item on the list using the same grammatical form.

No: All employees will receive *lifetime memberships* at Disco Dynasty, *weekend passes* to the movies, and *spend $50.00 gift certificates* at their favorite fast-food place.

Yes: All employees will receive *lifetime memberships* to Disco Dynasty, *weekend passes* to the movies, and *$50.00 gift certificates* for their favorite fast-food place.

No: A recent survey of employees indicates that they like working for Arc Electronics because it *provides generous benefits, job security is offered, and professional growth.* [None of the items in the list is in the same grammatical form.]

Yes: A recent survey of employees indicates that they like working for Arc Electronics because it

1. *provides* generous benefits,

2. *offers* job security, and

3. *encourages* professional growth.

Which One Doesn't Fit?

1. Lifetime memberships
2. Weekend passes
3. Spend $50.00 gift certificates

Spend $50.00 gift certificates isn't parallel because it begins with a verb and the other two do not.

4.6.1

No: We have to decide between *inputting* the highly-sensitive raw data ourselves or *hire* an outside firm to do it.

Yes: We have to decide between *inputting* the highly-sensitive raw data ourselves or *hiring* an outside firm to do it.

Use Lists

To add clarity to your writing and to emphasize items in a series, use lists. Clearly number, letter, or bullet the different items in your list, and set up these items in parallel form.

4.6
DANGLING OR MISPLACED MODIFIERS

Dangling or misplaced modifiers are words that are separated from the idea they are describing. There are two ways to correct dangling or misplaced modifiers.

4.6.1 Move the misplaced part of the sentence next to the word it modifies

No: She sold posture chairs to the secretaries with built-in padding. [In this sentence, the secretaries have built-in padding.]

Yes: She sold posture chairs with built-in padding to the secretaries.

4.6.2 Rewrite the sentence to make the reference clear

4.6.2

No: Being lost and confused, the police officer helped the little boy. [Here, the police officer is lost and confused.]

Yes: Because the boy was lost and confused, the police-officer helped him find his way.

Three Grammatical Niceties

Double negatives equal a positive. *He was not unclear in his instructions* means *his instructions were clear*. Avoid double negatives.

Prepositions at the end of sentences can make a sentence sound flat—*Marketing is what he took his degree in*. To avoid dangling the preposition *in* at the end of the sentence, rewrite the sentence—*He took his degree in marketing*. Remember, however, that this is not a rule, for sometimes the prepositional ending seems the most natural way to express an idea—*She is a woman who can be counted on*. This is more natural sounding and, therefore, preferable to the rewrite: *She is a woman on whom one can count*.

Split infinitives occur when words are placed between *to* and the *verb*. (The *to* form of the verb—*to search, to identify*—is called the infinitive.) Split infinitives should be avoided—*The investigators began to search the room thoroughly* (not *to thoroughly search*). *The anthropologists were able to identify definitely the remains in the cave* (not *to definitely identify*).

Punctuating Properly

Correct punctuation can make your writing easier to read. Though some people suggest that the best rule for punctuation is "when in doubt, leave it out," the careful writer follows a wiser rule: "When in doubt, look it up." The following guidelines give you a brief and useful reference when you must look up a particular punctuation mark.

5.1.2

5.1

THE COMMA (,)

5.1.1 Use commas between items in a series

Yes: He brought a calculator, a lap-top computer, and a cellular telephone to the office party.

While some grammarians and most journalists say that the comma before the "and" is unnecessary, using a comma will always keep the items clearly separate and improve readability.

5.1.2 Use a comma after an introductory expression

An introductory expression is a word, phrase, or clause that comes before the first subject of the sentence.

Yes: Moreover [a word], we feel confident that our staff meetings would not exceed one hour.

Yes: After discussing the problem with our manager [a phrase], we felt confident that our staff meetings would not exceed one hour.

Yes: After we discussed the problem with our manager [a clause], we felt confident that our staff meetings would not exceed one hour.

5.2.1

5.1.3 Use a comma before *and, but, for, nor, or, so,* and *yet* when they connect two *complete* sentences

No: Both sides found the negotiations difficult, but were able to compromise. [*"Were able to compromise"* is not a complete sentence.]

Yes: Both sides found the negotiations difficult but were able to compromise.

Yes: Both sides found the negotiations difficult, but they were able to compromise.

5.1.4. Place commas around expressions that interrupt the flow of the sentence

Yes: Apparently, despite what we have heard, he is going to be promoted to supervisor.

Yes: We met on April 17, 19__, to discuss access rights to beaches. [*The year is considered an interrupter and is set off by commas when it follows the month and day.*]

Yes: Please send this to Jan Doty, Personnel Director, Humungous Oil, P.O. Box 751, Midway, ND 85731.

5.2

THE SEMICOLON (;)

5.2.1 Use a semicolon between two closely related sentences

Connect two closely related complete sentences with a semicolon.

No: A woman swam across the Molokai Channel yesterday; there is life on Mars. [*The two ideas are not closely related.*]

Yes: A woman swam across the Molokai Channel yesterday; she set a new record.

No: The chair was too low for the workstation, therefore, she experienced lower back pain.

Yes: The chair was too low for the workstation; therefore, she experienced lower back pain.

5.3.1

5.2.2 Use a semicolon with conjunctive adverbs such as "therefore" and "however" when used between two *complete* sentences

Some Conjunctive Adverbs	
also	moreover
consequently	next
finally	still
furthermore	then
however	therefore
meanwhile	thus

5.2.3 Use a semicolon with items in a series when the items have commas within them

Yes: Attending the meeting were Gloria Cook, a member of the review board; Jonathan Chew, the Division Manager; and Lori Esteban, the employee representative.

5.3

THE COLON (:)

5.3.1 Use a colon after a complete statement to introduce a list, quotation, or title

No: In the back of the van were: a dozen beach mats, two surfboards, and a cooler of passion-fruit juice. [*In the back of the van were* is not a complete sentence.]

Yes: In the back of the van were a dozen beach mats, two surfboards, and a cooler of passion-fruit juice.

Yes: The following items were in the back of the van: a dozen beach mats, two surfboards, and a cooler of passion-fruit juice.

No: Section 15 of Contract No. 12345, "Agreement for Professional Services," states:
Confidentiality. All information given to the CONTRACTOR under this agreement shall be confidential and not made available to any person or organization by the CONTRACTOR without prior written approval of the COMPANY.

Yes: Section 15 of Contract No. 12345, "Agreement for Professional Services," states the following:
All information given to the CONTRACTOR under this agreement shall be confidential and not made available to any person or organization by the CONTRACTOR without prior written approval of the COMPANY.

(When quoting passages in a separate, indented paragraph, quotation marks are not necessary.)

5.3.2 Use a colon after a heading

To: James Smithson
      Land and Natural Resources Department

(*To* is the heading.)

5.4

THE PERIOD (.)

Place a period at the end of a sentence and after most abbreviations.

Use only one period when an abbreviation comes at the end of the sentence.

Yes: Please tell Ms. Rodrigues that the consultants are from Island Construction, Inc.

5.5

THE APOSTROPHE (')

5.5.1 To show possession of a singular noun, use the apostrophe and "s"

Yes: He appreciated the **attorney's** free advice.

Yes: The Governor encouraged the **child's** questions.

5.5.2 To show possession of a singular noun ending in "s," add the apostrophe and "s" or only the apostrophe

Yes: I gave **James's** (or **James'**) report to the committee.

5.5.3 To show possession of a plural noun ending in "s," add only the apostrophe

Yes: He appreciated the three **attorneys'** free advice.

5.5.4. For plural words not ending in "s," use the apostrophe and "s"

Yes: The Governor encouraged the **children's** questions.

5.5.5 To form plurals, use either the apostrophe and "s" or just "s"

the **1900's** or the **1900s**

their **BMW's** or their **BMWs**

all **B's** or all **Bs**

5.5.6 When combining words, use an apostrophe where letters have been omitted

are not = aren't	I would = I'd
cannot = can't	it is = it's
could have = could've	she will = she'll
have not = haven't	they have = they've
he is = he's	were not = weren't
I am = I'm	you are = you're

Avoid contractions in formal writing. In less formal writing, negative contractions such as "don't" and "isn't" are often used because the negative is much clearer to the reader.

5.6

THE QUOTATION MARKS ("")

Use quotation marks around a direct quotation, the title of a short work or report, and words used in a special sense, such as puns or slang.

Yes: "Tom," she said, "let's go body surfing at North Beach."

Yes: To understand the situation, read the Department of Health and Human Services' report, "The Changing Needs of the Nation's Aging Citizens."

Yes: The angry hospital cook did a "slow burn."

Periods and commas are always placed inside the quotation marks as in the preceding examples.

Colons and semicolons are always outside the quotation marks.

The manager asked about "down time"; the supervisor told the manager more than she wanted to hear.

Question marks and exclamation points are placed inside the quotation marks when the quotation marks apply to the entire quotation.

The Marketing Manager asked, "What is truth?"

Question marks and exclamation points appear outside the final quotation marks when they apply to the entire sentence.

What is "truth"? ["Truth" is only part of the sentence; therefore, the question mark is placed after the quotation mark.]

5.7

THE PARENTHESES (())

5.7.1 Use parentheses to insert extra information that your reader might want to know

Yes: He was a social services investigator for over 30 years (1950-1980) and never missed a day of work.

Yes: Plea bargaining (see page 67) was developed to speed the judicial process.

5.7.2 No terminal punctuation or capitalization is needed for a complete sentence within parentheses

Yes: You are a careful writer (we know this because you bought the book, and you are reading the preface).

5.8

THE DASH (- - OR ——)

Use a dash to indicate an abrupt change of thought or to clarify what follows. In most writing (there are exceptions in journalistic writing), there are no spaces between the dash and the words which immediately precede and succeed it.

Yes: We hope he goes far—very far.

Yes: It isn't often—maybe twice a year—that I am asked to speak before a large audience.

Note: On most typewriters and some computers, the dash is created by typing two hyphens (--). Most word processing programs and computer printers now include the dash (—) on the keyboard.

When to Dash

Remember that the dash is considered an informal punctuation mark and should not be used in very formal writing. Dashes increase the emphasis on the information that follows. Parentheses reduce the emphasis on the information enclosed within them and are found in both formal and informal writing.

5.9

THE HYPHEN (-)

Use a hyphen to express the idea of a unit and to avoid ambiguity.

Yes: She took the Dallas-Fort Worth shuttle every morning, sipping her heavily sugared coffee on the flight. [Adverbs, like *heavily* in this sentence are rarely followed by a hyphen.]

Yes: We are experiencing a small-shipment problem. [The *small-shipment* is a type of shipment problem.]
We are experiencing a small shipment problem. [The *shipment problem* is *small*.]

5.10

THE ELLIPSIS (. . .)

5.10.1 Use ellipsis when part of a sentence has been omitted

An ellipsis mark indicates that you have left something out of a quoted passage.

Original: As I'd learned from McNamara, the discipline of writing something down is the first step toward making it happen. In conversation, you can get away with all kinds of vagueness and nonsense, often without realizing it. But there's something about putting your thoughts on paper that forces you to get down to specifics. That way, it's harder to deceive yourself—or anybody else. (*Iacocca: An Autobiography*, Lee Iacocca with William Novak)

Edited: ... the discipline of writing something down is the first step toward making it happen. In conversation, you can get away with all kinds of vagueness and nonsense, often without realizing it. But there's something about putting your thoughts on paper that forces you to get down to specifics. That way, it's harder to deceive yourself—or anybody else.

5.10.2 Use ellipsis when sentences have been omitted

Indicate the final punctuation mark of the previous sentence if it is important; then include the ellipsis.

Edited: ... the discipline of writing something down is the first step toward making it happen. . . . there's something about putting your thoughts on paper that forces you to get down to specifics. That way, it's harder to deceive yourself—or anybody else.

5.10.3 Include the final punctuation mark if the ellipsis appears at the end of a sentence

Edited: . . . the discipline of writing something down is the first step toward making it happen. . . . there's something about putting your thoughts on paper that forces you to get down to specifics. That way, it's harder to deceive yourself. . . .

Keeping Mechanics Consistent

6

6

When do you capitalize "president"? Do you write out "21"? Are titles of reports underlined? Can you divide "open" if it comes at the end of a line? Is it "commitment" or "committment"? The answers to these questions come under the general heading of mechanics—the "humbug" of writing. These guidelines will help you with the common problems.

6.1

CAPITALIZATION

6.1.1 First letter of a sentence

Capitalize the first letter of a sentence.

All administrative assistants were asked to develop contingency plans.

6.1.2 First letter of a quoted sentence

Capitalize the first letter of a quoted sentence unless the quotation blends into the rest of the sentence.

The President said, "**T**his is an idea for tomorrow that we must start planning for today."

The Governor spoke of "an idea for tomorrow that we must start planning for today."

6.1.3 Proper nouns

Capitalize proper (specific) nouns but not common (nonspecific) nouns.

PROPER NOUN	COMMON NOUN
God	a god
Business Studies Center	a study center
University of Nebraska	a state university
Department of Corrections	a state department
The State Capitol	a state building
The State of Maine	a state in the north east*

6.1.5

6.1.4 Titles as part of a proper name

Capitalize titles of persons when used as part of a proper name.

King George

Representative Ramirez

Captain Horner

Judge Ikeda

6.1.5 Titles of public officials

Capitalize titles of public officials when the titles are used alone to refer to the specific person.

The President stopped at Andrews Air Force Base on his way to Brazil.

---

*Capitalize the word **state** when it specifically refers to the political unit but not when it refers to the geographical unit. The State of Maine, therefore, refers to the state government of Maine. The state of Maine refers to the land mass.

We asked the **Governor** to speak at the awards banquet. He was among seven state **governors** who had been given special recognition this year.

6.1.6 Job titles for high rank

Job titles indicating high rank or distinction may be capitalized when they refer to a specific person.

The Adjutant General was happy to hear that **a judge, a state representative, the President of Browning Corp.**, and **the Board Chairperson of Walston Company** would also be serving on the board.

6.2
ABBREVIATIONS

6.2.1 Titles before or after names

Abbreviate titles immediately before or after proper names

Lt. Gov. Samuelson	or	John Samuelson, **Jr.**
Dr. Louise Wilson	or	Louise Wilson, **M.D.**
Rep. Gayle Kennedy	or	Gayle Kennedy, **J.D.**
Mr. Mark Ward	or	Mark Ward, **Lt. Col.**

6.2.2 Names of organizations, programs, and materials

Abbreviate names of organizations, programs, and materials after their first spelled out appearance.

Personnel officers from the Department of Human Services (**DHS**) and the Department of Personnel Services (**DPS**) met to discuss their administrative needs.

The Board of Directors (**the Board**) met to discuss the effects on sales of the North American Free Trade Agreement (**NAFTA**) and the General Agreement on Tariffs and Trade (**GATT**).

Don't Over-Abbreviate

The boxes weighed nine pounds. (Not **lbs.**)

The employee committee met in January, March, and April. (Not **Jan., Mar.,** and **Apr.**)

Poor: New releases of NCP, VSE, and VM will be installed in DPC. The changes in VSE 2.1 are probably the most dramatic since the OS environment was made available to the CICS bases. [Even though these initializations may have been spelled out earlier in the writing, there are too many in this paragraph for the nontechnical reader.]

6.3

NUMBERS

6.3.1 Less than ten

Spell out all numbers less than ten.

Jack carried **two** trays of sushi to the manager's office.

Suddenly, **75** excited school children descended on our office.

6.3.2 Beginning sentences

6.3.4

Spell out all numbers that begin sentences.

Ninety-six of the employees wanted to enroll in the new pension plan.

If a large number such as 1,156 begins the sentence, rewrite the sentence so that the number is not the first word.

6.3.3 Two or more in a list

When two or more numbers are used together in a list and one of the numbers is above nine, use numerals for all the numbers.

The list included **5** from Maui, **6** from Kauai, and **21** from Oahu.

6.3.4 Dates, addresses, percentages, fractions, decimals, statistics, money, time, and ID numbers

Use numerals for dates, addresses, percentages, fractions, decimals, statistics, exact amounts of money, time, and identification numbers.

Date:	August 21, 1999
Address:	830 Locust Street
Percentage:	60 percent
Fraction:	1/2
Decimal:	.075
Statistic:	6 out of 100
Exact amount of money:	$275.22
Time:	5:00 p.m.
Identification number:	575-75-7575

6.4

ITALICS (UNDERLINING)

6.4.1 Titles

Italicize or underline the titles of books, plays, films, long poems, musical compositions, magazines, newspapers, pamphlets, and long reports.

> To ensure that we accurately apply the restrictions, please read Sections 8 and 52 of <u>Internal Revenue Service: Taxing Your Almighty Dollar.</u>

6.4.2 Ships, trains, planes, and spacecraft

Italicize or underline the names of ships, trains, planes, and spacecraft.

> The student applied to NASA to ride *Adventurer III* to the moon.

6.4.3 Emphasis

Italics or underlining may be used to emphasize ideas.

> It was not the third but the *fourth* time this week that he came in early to work.

Don't Overuse Italics or Underlining for Emphasis

No: The woman said she was *so* tired she *couldn't* think straight.

6.5

WORD DIVISION

6.5.1 Between syllables

Avoid dividing a word at the end of a line—divide between syllables and never divide one syllable words.

No: *sour- ce*

Yes: pre- fer

Yes: plan- ning

6.5.2 Not between single letters

Never divide a word if a single letter would stand alone at the end of the line.

No: o- pen

No: T- shirt

6.5.3 In compound words

Divide all compound words (two words read as one) after the first word.

Yes cost- efficient

Yes cross- examine

6.5.4 With dates, abbreviations, numbers, and contractions

Do not divide dates, abbreviations, numbers, and con- tractions.

6.5.5

No: January- 1

No: DH-HS

No: 2,201,- 123

No: could- n't

6.5.5 With names

Do not divide names, if possible.

No: Mrs.- Jennifer Young

No: Mr. Michael- Tripp

Sometimes, however, a very long name will appear at the end of the line. In this case, divide after the first name, never after the title.

Spelling

Commitment or Committment?

Spelling errors reduce your credibility as a writer. Even if your computer has a "spell-check," keep a dictionary handy, or find a coworker to proofread your writing. Whatever technique you choose, don't use the excuse, "Well, it looks okay—" Look it up!

Commitment

Using Words Correctly

A

This guide lists some of the more commonly confused and misused words and phrases. It also includes words which are frequently used in writing but are considered either overly formal and pompous or too informal and substandard.

a, an. Use **a** before a word that begins with a consonant sound—*I sent a letter to the Senator.* Use **an** before a word that begins with a vowel sound—*It was an appreciation of his good work.* In words which begin with *h*, use **a** if you sound the *h*: a hospital, a hotel. If you do not sound the *h*, use **an**: an heir, an honest deed.

accept, except. Accept is a verb which means *to receive*—*I accepted the award on behalf of my entire department.* **Except** is usually a preposition indicating exclusion—*Everyone brought food to the celebration except me.*

advice, advise. Advice is a noun which means *information offered*; **advise** is a verb meaning *to give an opinion*—*My advice to you is not to advise the supervisor on actions he should take.*

affect, effect. Affect is generally a verb meaning *to influence*; **effect** is most often a noun meaning *result*—*The gossip affected us in several ways, and the effect was disastrous.* **Effect** is sometimes a verb which means *to bring about*—*The hurricane effected dramatic changes in our services.*

agree to, agree with. When you **agree to** something, you give consent—*We agreed to meet in the Vice President's office at 3:00 p.m. Friday.* When you **agree with** someone or something, you come to an agreement with that person or thing—*In this case, the social worker agreed with the parents, not the judge.*

a lot, alot. A lot is two words. **Alot** is not a word. **A lot** is also considered informal and should be avoided in most writing.

all right, alright. Use **all right; alright** is substandard—*The job looked all right to me.*

alternative, option. Alternative includes two choices; **option** involves more than two choices—*Neither alternative, either eating in my office or in the very cold lunchroom, was appealing. So I looked for a third option.*

among, between. Among is used with three or more elements; **between** is used with two—*Between the two of them, John is the faster typist. Among the three of them, Mark is the fastest typist.*

amount, number. Use **amount** for quantities you cannot count—*The amount of paper we use in this office is incredible.* Use **number** for those quantities you can count—*Of all the departments in the company, we had the greatest number of people absent after the Fourth of July weekend.*

an. See *a, an.*

and/or. And/or is an awkward construction used mostly in legal or very technical documents. Writers should avoid the expression in letters and memos. Instead, write *John or Bill, or both, will attend.*

anxious, eager. Both words mean *desirous* or *wishing.* There is, however, an element of fear and anxiety in **anxious**—*I was eager* [not anxious] *to hear her speech.*

as. As can mean both *because* and *when.* If there is a possibility that the reader might confuse these meanings, avoid **as**—*We left the meeting because* [not *as*] *the participants started yelling at each other.* [In this sentence, **as** could mean *when* and *because.*]

A

as, like. As connects two complete ideas; **like** does not—*He works for Acme Auto as his cousin does.* [Not *like his cousin does.*] *The perfume smells like roses.*

assure. See *ensure, insure.*

being as, being that. These are substandard. Use **because** or **since.**

between. See *among, between.*

biannual, biennial, semiannual. Biannual and **semiannual** mean *twice a year;* **biennial** is *once every two years* or *continuing for two years.* Because these words are confusing, simply write *twice a year* or *once every two years.*

can, may. Can refers to ability—*Can you complete the monthly report by noon?* **May** refers to permission—*May I call you at 11 a.m. to see how you are doing on the report?*

capital, capitol. Capitol refers only to a building—*The State Capitol is located in the center of town.* **Capital** is used to refer to everything else.
❏ *The capital of Illinois is Springfield.*
❏ *We have five million dollars in the capital improvement fund.*
❏ *The State Legislature discusses capital punishment every session.*
❏ *When you write "Harry," you always begin with a capital "H."*

censor, censure. Censor is *to remove morally and politically objectionable material*—*The material was censored before it left the office.* **Censure** is *to disapprove*—*The employee was censured by his coworkers because of his sexist remarks.*

compare, contrast. Compare discusses both similarities and differences; **contrast** involves only differences.

complement, compliment. Complement, as a verb, means *to go together well with something;* as a noun,

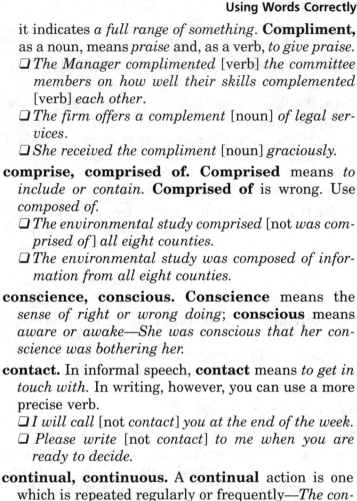

it indicates *a full range of something*. **Compliment,** as a noun, means *praise* and, as a verb, *to give praise.*

❑ *The Manager complimented* [verb] *the committee members on how well their skills complemented* [verb] *each other.*

❑ *The firm offers a complement* [noun] *of legal services.*

❑ *She received the compliment* [noun] *graciously.*

comprise, comprised of. Comprised means *to include or contain.* **Comprised of** is wrong. Use *composed of.*

❑ *The environmental study comprised* [not *was comprised of*] *all eight counties.*

❑ *The environmental study was composed of information from all eight counties.*

conscience, conscious. Conscience means the *sense of right or wrong doing*; **conscious** means *aware or awake—She was conscious that her conscience was bothering her.*

contact. In informal speech, **contact** means *to get in touch with.* In writing, however, you can use a more precise verb.

❑ *I will call* [not *contact*] *you at the end of the week.*

❑ *Please write* [not *contact*] *to me when you are ready to decide.*

continual, continuous. A **continual** action is one which is repeated regularly or frequently—*The continual clamor of the pile driver was maddening.* A **continuous** action is one without interruption—*The road from Elko to Salt Lake City is a continuous stretch of asphalt.*

contrast. See *compare, contrast.*

could of. Could of in place of the contraction **could've** is wrong. Use **could have** in professional writing. *I could have gone if asked.*

council, counsel. A **council** is *a governing body—We will present this plan to the council at the next meet-*

ing. To **counsel** is *to give advice—He received good counsel from the personnel manager.*

criteria, criterion. Criteria is plural. **Criterion** is singular.

data. While many people insist that **data** can only be used as plural—*The data are ready for analysis*—others use it as either singular or plural—*The data is ready for analysis.* This is a matter of choice. **Datum,** in Latin, the singular form of **data,** is not very common and should be avoided.

differ from, differ with. Differ from indicates contrast—*This emergency defense system differs from the previous system on several major points.* **Differ with** indicates disagreement—*The Captain differed with the Colonel on how the National Guard should be deployed.*

disinterested, uninterested. To be **disinterested** means *to be impartial—He was a disinterested judge of the case.* To be **uninterested** is *to be not interested—He was uninterested in the squabbling between the two parties.*

eager. See *anxious, eager.*

effect. See *affect, effect.*

e.g. E.g. means *exempli gratia* or *for example.* Avoid this expression in formal writing. Work your examples smoothly into the sentence—*His request included such office items as paper clips, rubber bands, and staples.* (Also see *i.e.*)

elicit, illicit. To **elicit** is *to draw out;* **illicit** is *illegal or immoral—The testimony he elicited from the witness made us all realize we were dealing with illicit acts.*

emigrate, immigrate. To **emigrate** is *to leave a country or geographical area—Many people have emigrated from Southeast Asia since the end of the*

Vietnam War. **To immigrate** is *to settle in another country—People have immigrated to Los Angeles from all parts of the world.*

eminent, imminent. Eminent means *distinguished—He was an eminent statesman before retiring to teach at the University of Virginia.* **Imminent** means *about to happen—She awaited the imminent arrival of the movie star.*

ensure, insure. Most dictionaries treat these words as interchangeable. Some writers, however, always use **assure** with people—*Please assure me that you will be there on time.* They use **ensure** with things—*We fill out all of the forms to ensure that the request goes through.* They use **insure** with money *(The mainframe computer was insured for $350,000.)* Most American writers use **insure** when referring to insurance.

etc. Etc., an abbreviation of **et cetera**, means *and so forth.* Avoid this expression in formal writing. Instead, rewrite your sentence and show that your list is not inclusive—*Please bring with you all the relevant documents including bills, receipts, I.O.U. notes, and bank statements.*

except. See *accept, except.*

farther, further. Farther is used with physical distances—*The trip from Denver to Minneapolis was farther than I expected.* Use **further** for everything else—*If you want to pursue this matter further, please talk to my boss.*

female, male; women, men. Female and male are used to make biological distinctions in scientific writing. They should not be used interchangeably with *women* and *men—Five men* [not *males*] *and six women* [not *females*] *stood in line for their checks.*

fewer, less. Use **fewer** with quantities that can be counted; use **less** with amounts which cannot— *Fewer people than expected attended the ceremonies. This was all right because there was less food to eat this year.*

firstly. This expression, used in **firstly, secondly, thirdly,** is considered outdated. Use **first, second, third** instead.

flammable, inflammable. Both mean *easily burned* or *ignited.* However, because readers often think **inflammable** means unburnable, use **flammable.**

further. See *farther, further.*

got. Got is not a replacement for *was* or *have—He was* [not *got*] *fired.* In the expression *has got* or *have got,* **got** can usually be eliminated—*I have* [not *have got*] *a week to move to my new office.*

hanged, hung. Hanged refers to executions—*The prisoner was hanged at dawn.* **Hung** refers to something that has been fastened or suspended—*The keys were hung on the hook by the door.*

he/she, him/her. These awkward expressions should be avoided. Use the plural or rewrite the idea. Don't write: *Each of them wrote to say that he / she found the computer program very useful.* Write: *All of them wrote to say that they found the computer program very useful.*

hopefully. Hopefully means *full of hope—The departmental reorganization will help us look hopefully to the future.* It does not mean *I hope.* Don't write: *Hopefully, it will help us plan wisely for the future.*

hung. See *hanged, hung.*

i.e. I.e. means **id est** or *that is.* Avoid this expression in formal writing. Work your example smoothly into the sentence. *The two offices,* [not *i.e.*] *the Claims Section and the Permit Bureau, are on the top floor.* (See also *e.g.*)

if, whether. Use **if** to express condition—*If you need further information, please call me at 548-1234.* Use **whether** to express alternatives—*Right now, the key question is whether we should build the crisis center in Seattle or in Tacoma.*

illicit. See *elicit, illicit.*

immigrate. See *emigrate, immigrate.*

imminent. See *eminent, imminent.*

impact. Impact means *result* and is most often a singular, collective noun—*We studied the impact of the new housing project on the community.* Avoid using the plural form of **impact**. Not: *We studied various impacts of the development on the community.* Also, avoid **impact** as a verb—*The new project has affected* [not *impacted*] *delivery systems.*

imply, infer. To imply means *to suggest—While she did not state it, her comments implied that our office was involved.* **To infer** is to *draw a conclusion— Though there were no witnesses, the facts allowed us to infer that the lock on the file cabinet had been jimmied.*

in, into. Use **in** to show location or condition; use **into** to show movement—*The notes for the speech she was about to deliver were in her husband's pocket, and he had just gone into the men's room.*

individual. Individual used for person or people is pompous—*Six people* [not *individuals*] *were given letters of commendation for their fine work.*

infer. See *imply, infer.*

inflammable. See *flammable, inflammable.*

in regards to. This expression is substandard for *regarding, in regard to, with regard to,* and *as regards.* Use one of the four instead of **in regards to** or eliminate the phrase.

No: In regards to the previous directive, ignore it.

Yes: Ignore the previous directive.

L

insure. See *ensure, insure.*

inter, intra. Inter refers to something which connects or involves two or more elements—*The two Governors discussed methods to improve interstate commerce.* **Intra** refers to connections within the boundaries of a single element—*The new intrastate airline will fly from Lawton to Red Hill.*

into. See *in, into.*

irregardless. This expression is incorrect. **Regardless** should be used.

its, it's. Its shows possession—*The department cannot function smoothly without its dedicated support staff.* **It's** combines *it* and *is* **or** *it* **and** *has*—**It's** [it is] *time everyone took seriously what the boss said.* **It's** [it has] *been a positive experience.*

later, latter. Later means *after the proper time* or *at some time in the future*—*The computer arrived later than we had expected. He will work later this week.* **Latter** is *the second of two things mentioned*—*Your latter suggestion is more likely to be adopted.*

lay. Lay, as a present tense verb, means *to place*—*Every morning, I lay my briefcase on top of my desk.* **Lay,** as a past tense verb, means *to recline*—*I lay under the coconut tree awaiting enlightenment.*

lead, led. Lead is a noun indicating a *soft malleable metal.* **Led** is the past tense of the verb *to lead. She led the race carrying 50 pounds of lead in her backpack.*

less. See *fewer, less.*

liable, likely. Liable refers to consequences that are undesirable—*He is liable to repeat the error.* It also indicates legal responsibility—*She is liable for damages.* Use **likely** when referring to desirable consequences—*She is likely to enjoy her new position.*

like. See *as, like.*

likely. See *liable, likely.*

loose, lose. Loose, as an adjective, means *not to be securely fastened.* **Lose,** as a verb, means *to misplace* or *to not win. He will lose his pants because his belt is loose.*

male. See *female, male.*

mankind. Use *people, humanity, humans, the human race,* or *humankind.*

may. See *can, may.*

may be, maybe. May be is a verb phrase—*We may be able to give you a ride home to Bennington.* **Maybe** is an adverb—*Maybe, we can meet for dinner after the staff meeting.*

media, medium. Media is plural. It can mean *representatives of the media—The media were helpful in spreading the word about the epidemic.* Media can also refer to *the means by which a message is carried. She uses several media in her work: oil, clay, and glass.* **Medium** is singular—*Television will be the primary medium for promoting the new energy program.*

Miss, Mrs., Ms. Miss is a title referring to an unmarried woman or young girl. The abbreviation **Mrs.** (for Mistress) is used with married women. **Ms.** is used for married and unmarried women in all cases except when **Miss** or **Mrs.** is preferred. Both **Ms.** (with a period) and **Ms** (without the period) are correct.

number. See *amount, number.*

option. See *alternative, option.*

oral, spoken, verbal. While most people do not make a distinction between **oral, spoken,** and **verbal,** a difference does exist. **Oral** and **spoken** refer only to speech. **Verbal** means expressed by word—both written and spoken. When you are told, *"You need only a verbal agreement,"* this could mean a written agreement.

passed, past. Passed is a verb meaning *to move beyond something—He passed me on the freeway going 90 miles an hour.* **Past** as a noun, refers to *history—He thought fondly of the past.* **Past,** as an adjective, means *previous* or *earlier—In this past year, I lost twenty pounds.* **Past,** as an adverb, indicates *moving by or beyond—She tiptoed past the boss' office.*

percent, percentage. Percent is used with specific figures—*Almost 85 percent of the population supports the wildlife preservation plan.* **Percentage** is a descriptive word used with unspecified amounts—*A very small percentage of the population would like to turn South Point into a parking lot.*

❏ Avoid using the symbol % except in charts, graphs, or other visual aids.

❏ When a phrase beginning with *of* comes after **percent,** the verb usually agrees with the noun in the phrase—*Ninety percent of the **members are** in favor of the expansion.*

❏ When **percent** stands alone, it is singular—*Ninety percent is in favor of the expansion.*

phenomena, phenomenon. Phenomena is the plural of **phenomenon.**

❏ *Many strange phenomena occur regularly in our building.*

❏ *That the water fountain does not work every time I need a drink is a strange phenomenon.*

precede, proceed. Precede means *to come before;* **proceed** means *to continue—This historian proceeded to explain how it might have been possible for another group of people to have preceded the Polynesians to Hawaii.*

P

principal, principle. A **principle** is a law, guideline, or rule of conduct—*She was a politician of the highest principles.* **Principal** is used for everything else.
❑ *When I was attending elementary school, the principal was my pal.*
❑ *The principal reason I am reading this is to understand how to use words correctly.*
❑ *The principal on the loan for my Georgetown home will be repaid in thirty years.*

proceed. See *precede, proceed.*

raise, rise. **Raise** means *to lift or move something upward*—*She slowly raised her head from the table and asked what had happened.* **Rise** means *to move upward*—*His hair actually started to rise when he saw the revised figures for the freeway construction.*

reason is because. This expression is wrong. Use **that** instead of **because**—*The reason I arrived late for work is that I had a flat tire on Market Street.*

reason why. In this expression, **why** is redundant—*The reason* [not *the reason* why] *the bill did not pass the House of Representatives is obvious.*

relation, relationship. **Relation** shows a connection between things—*The public wants to know the relation between tourism and the economy.* **Relationship** makes a connection between people—*The relationship between our office staff and theirs is very friendly.*

rise. See *raise, rise.*

semiannual. See *biannual, biennial.*

served, serviced. People are **served**—*The clerks at the window served* [not *serviced*] *an average of 200 people daily.* Things are **serviced**—*The technician serviced all of the adding machines in the building.*

set, sit. **Set** means *to put or arrange something*—*Despite my anger, I politely set the document on her* *desk.* **Sit** means *to be seated—Because he is long-winded, I sit the moment he walks into my office.*

shall, will. At one time, **shall** was used primarily with I and we—*I shall call you in a week.* That distinction is disappearing, and **shall** and **will** are used interchangeably. Most often today, **shall** appears in polite questions—*Shall I mail the report to you now?*—or in legal documents to show obligation—*This shall be filed before the end of the month.* **Will** is generally used in the future tense—*I will go tomorrow*—or in questions about the future—*When will you visit New York again?*

spoken. See *oral, spoken, verbal.*

stationary, stationery. Stationary means *in a fixed position;* **stationery** means *writing paper and envelopes—She stood stationary as I yelled, "Where's the new stationery?"*

than, then. Than is used to show contrast—*The money required to complete the renovations was more than I expected.* **Then** refers to time—*The next step, then, is to find the money for this project.*

that. See *where* and *which.*

that, where. Avoid using **where** in place of **that**—*I see that* [not *where*] *we will have to increase our productivity while we cut staff positions.*

that, which. That introduces a clause that is essential to the meaning of the sentence—*Her condo had a large window that looked directly at Mount Rushmore.* [Her condo may have had many windows, but this was a large window that looked directly at Mount Rushmore.] **Which** introduces a clause that provides additional, not essential, information. The **which** clause is almost always set off by commas—*Her condo had one window, which looked directly at Mount Rushmore.* [Her condo had only one window.]

W

that, who. **That** is only used with people who are viewed as a group or anonymous—*Infants that cry should be cuddled.* **Who** is generally used with people—*The people we enjoy working with are those who* [not *that*] *display a positive attitude.* **Who** may refer to animals when they have names—*My cat Toby, who ate all my goldfish, died recently.*

their, there, they're. **Their** is the possessive pronoun. **There** indicates *location.* **They're** is the contraction for *they are—They're going to miss their meeting if they aren't there in one minute.*

to, too, two. **To** is a preposition showing direction. **Too** means *in addition* or *also.* **Two** refers to the number—*She, too, went to speak to the Vice-President about the two available managerial positions.*

try and. This expression is substandard. Use **try to**—*Management and labor should try to* [not *try and*] *work together to reach a settlement.*

uninterested. See *disinterested, uninterested.*

unique. **Unique** means *singular* or *one of a kind.* Therefore, expressions such as "most unique," "very unique," or "more unique" are illogical. Something is either **unique** or it is not.

use to, used to. Use **used to**—*He used to* [not *use to*] *attend meetings regularly.*

verbal. See *oral, spoken, verbal.*

wait for, wait on. **Wait for** means *to await—I waited for Steven for almost 20 minutes.* **Wait on** means *to serve—My boss told me that I would probably have to wait on about 50 clients per day.*

whether. See *if, whether.*

who, whom. **Who** is always a subject; **whom** is always an object. If the **w** word is followed by a verb, it is probably **who**—*Ms. Souza, who was always the first to volunteer for community work, has taken a*

W

job with a nonprofit agency. [*Who* is the subject of the verb *was.*] If the **w** word is followed by a noun or pronoun, use **whom**—*The people whom we have asked for help in our child abuse program are ready to begin the fund-raising compaign.* [*We,* not *whom,* is the subject of the verb phrase *have asked for help.*]

will. See *shall, will.*

women, men. See *female, male.*

would of. **Would of** in place of the contraction **would've** is substandard. Use **would have** in professional writing—*He would have resigned if his request were denied.*

your, you're. **Your** is the possessive pronoun. **You're** is the contraction for *you are—You're going to be a homeowner once your mortgage loan is approved.*

More Than a Question of Usage: Use Gender Free Language

1. Don't make unnecessary gender distinctions.

No: The Engineering Department advertised for a couple of women to act as receptionists.

Yes: The Engineering Department advertised for two receptionists.

2. Rewrite sentences to delete sexist pronouns.

No: **Each** employee must have **his** physical examination once a year.

Yes: **Each** employee must have **a** physical examination once a year. [Delete the pronoun and, if necessary, replace it with "a," "an," or "the."]

Yes: **All** employees must take **their** physical examination. [Change all the appropriate nouns, pronouns, or verbs to the plural.]

Avoid the awkward "his or her" unless absolutely necessary.

Formatting Your Message

8.1

Part of a written message's appeal to the reader is the way it looks on paper. Your ideas will be better received when your memos and letters have neat typing, white space, and visual balance. While there are many ways to format a message, the following guidelines will help you standardize your writing.

8.1

THE MEMO FORMAT

The memo format is used for messages sent within a company and for informal messages sent between companies. A sample memo is found on page 115.

8.1.1 Margins

Margins should be between one and two inches and equal on both sides of the page. (The sample memo does not reflect those proportions.)

Memorandum Line?

Many memos begin with a *Memorandum Line* that reads "Memo" or "Memorandum." Since the form of the memo indicates the type of communication it is, the memorandum line seems redundant. It should be avoided.

SAMPLE MEMO

C&R
MEMO

2 to 6 spaces

July 6, 19__   **Date**

Receiver's   *TO:*   Rosa R. Begum, Director
name   Human Resources   **Sender's**
2 spaces   **name**

        FROM: Special Committee on Employee Resignations
2 spaces

        SUBJECT: Final Report   **Subject line**

2 to 4 spaces

"Communication and Hugs: Attrition at C&R" presents the Special
Committee on Employee Resignations' findings concerning the high
attrition experienced at C&R in March, April, and May.

The report finds three main causes for this shock to the company's
system: 1) the various stresses caused by the relocation of the
company's main plant, 2) a perceived decrease in company benefits,
and 3) rumors generated by the recent management reorganization.

Overall, these were symptomatic of what we believe to be a
temporary disregard for employee communication brought on by the
relocation. To ensure that such a problem does not happen again, the
report makes two recommendations for action by the Department of
Human Resources.

For the committee, I am available at any time to discuss our
conclusions with you. My extension is 4739.

8.1.2 The date

The *date* is placed at the left margin and two to four spaces below the letterhead. [Spacing is adjusted to create a balanced look on the page.]

8.1.3 The receiver line

The *receiver line* (typed To:) is located two to six spaces below the date line and against the left margin. It includes the name of the person receiving the message and the title or department of that person on the next line.

8.1.4 The through line

If the memo is being sent through another person, a *through line* (typed Through:) with this person's name and title may be included. It is placed two spaces below the receiver line and against the left margin.

8.1.5 The sender line

The *sender line* (typed From:) is located two spaces below the receiver or through line and against the left margin. The person sending the memo signs or initials next to the name. If the memo has a signature block, there is no sender line.

8.1.6 The subject line

The *subject line* (typed Subject:) is placed two spaces below the sender line and flush against the left margin. It gives a precise description of the memo's content. The subject may be typed in capital letters to make it stand out from the body of the memo.

8.1.7 The body

The *body* begins two to four spaces below the subject line. The beginning of each *body* paragraph is not indented, and the text of the paragraph is single-spaced with double spacing between paragraphs.

8.1.9

8.1.8 Headings

Headings are often used within the body of memos and longer letters to guide the reader and break up the monotony of a densely typed page. A good heading is a short, descriptive title of a section. Avoid structural headings such as "Introduction," "Body," and "Conclusion." Use headings that speak to the reader:

I. Status of project

II. Actions to be taken

III. Revised timetable

Use *centered headings* for main points and *side headings* for secondary points. A side heading is placed flush with the left margin. If it is on its own line, it does not require a punctuation mark. If it is followed immediately by a sentence, place a colon or period after it.

8.1.9 The initials

The *initials* of the person writing or dictating the memo and of the typist are often included two spaces below the body. The initials of the person writing are in capital letters and followed by a colon. The typist's initials are in lower case letters (LL:mf).

8.2

8.1.10 The enclosure notation

The *enclosure notation* is located two spaces below the initials and flush with the left margin. It may be abbreviated Enc. and is followed by a numeral enclosed in parentheses, indicating the number of enclosures when there is more than one. If there are many enclosures and particularly if these need to be signed by the reader, identify them with a simple title following the "Enclosure."

8.1.11 The copy designation

The *copy designation* lists the names of people who will receive copies of the memo. It is a single "c" (c:) and is against the left margin, two spaces below the enclosure notation.

8.1.12 The second page heading

The *second page heading* is placed on the upper left corner of the second page, flush with the left margin. It is typed five to seven lines from the top of the page. On the first line is the reader's name; on the second line, the date; and on the third line, the number of the page (Page 2). The second page should include more than one sentence.

8.2

THE LETTER FORMAT

The letter format is used for formal intra- and inter-company writing and for all correspondence to the public. A sample letter is found on page 119.

SAMPLE LETTER

Chilton Chemical Clean-Up Company
Development Division
405-C Clearview Blvd.
Fair Plains, Nevada 39025

Date   April 27, 19__

2 to 4 spaces

Mr. Martin Cohn, President   **Inside**
Sparta Consumer Protective Association   **address**
157 South Coberg Street, Suite 118
Sparta, NC. 28316
2 to 4 spaces
Dear Mr. Cohn: **Salutation**
2 spaces
                    Subject: Chemical Study, Walden Pond   **Subject line**
2 to 4 spaces
Our proposed chemical study at Walden Pond has several goals. Primarily, it
will help us plan a clean up strategy for the area. It will also help us develop
survey strategies for other environmentally suspect areas. This, in turn, will
open new opportunities for other studies.

Chilton Chemical believes that the lead in the clean up of the project should
be taken by private industry. This will make industry both more
environmentally conscious and more careful.

The clean up of Walden Pond will become a reality because of the interest
and support of organizations such as yours. If I can be of additional help to
you, please call me at 722-1111. Thank you for sharing your views with us.

                    Complimentary
Sincerely.   **close**

4 spaces

William Gonzales, Director   **Sender's**
Marketing Department   **name and**
                               title
2 spaces

WC:lk   **Initials**

c: Wilson Smythe   **Copy**

8.2.4

8.2.1 The margins

The *margins* of a letter should frame the page. There should be as much space on the top of the page as on the bottom and as much on the left side as on the right.

8.2.2 The date

The *date* of the letter should be flush with the left margin and two to four spaces below the letterhead.

8.2.3 The inside address

The *inside address,* placed two to six spaces below the date, is flush with the left margin. It may include the following items, with each appearing on a separate line.

Name of the reader

Title of the reader

Office or department

Organization

Street address

City, state, and zip code

If the title of the receiver is short, it may appear on the same line as the receiver's name.

8.2.4 The attention line

The *attention line* is used when you want a particular person in the company to read your letter, but you don't know the person's name. Place the attention line two spaces below the inside address and flush with the left margin.

Attention: Purchasing Agent

If you know the name of your reader, include it in the inside address and do not use the attention line.

8.2.5 The salutations

Salutations such as *Dear Mr. Wong* or *Dear Jean* are located two spaces below the inside address or the attention line. When the salutation is addressed to a title and name, it is followed by a colon [*Dear Mrs. Wong:*]. When addressed to a first name, it is followed by a comma [*Dear David,*]. When the gender of the reader is unknown, use the complete name and a colon [*Dear Dale Hughes:*] If an attention line has been used, the salutation should be addressed to the entire company [*Dear Willard Feed Company:*].

8.2.6 The subject or reference line

A *subject* or *reference line* that presents the subject of the letter (typed Subject:) is placed two spaces below the salutation and is flush with the left margin. The subject may be typed in capital letters. While helpful to the reader, the subject line is optional.

8.2.7 The body

The *body* of the letter begins two spaces below the salutation or the subject line. Flush with the left margin, it is single-spaced within the paragraph and double-spaced between paragraphs.

8.2.8 The complimentary close

The *complimentary close,* located two spaces below the body, is flush with the left margin. The type of complimentary close is determined by the salutation.

Is It "Your Highness"?

If the reader is	Use
A child	"Dear Miss _" or "Dear Master _"
A woman	"Dear Ms. _" (unless you know of another preference)
Unknown	"Dear Personnel Manager" (the reader's title) "Dear Task Force" (Don't use "Gentlemen" or "Sir.")
The President	"Dear President _"
A cabinet officer	"Dear Secretary _"
A Supreme Court Justice	"Dear Justice _"
A member of Congress	"Dear Senator _" "Dear Representative _"
A U.S. ambas- sador	"Dear Ambassador _"
A foreign ambas- sador	"Your Excellency"
A governor	"Dear Governor _"
A lieutenant governor	"Dear Lieutenant Governor _"
A judge	"Dear Judge _"
A state officer	"Dear Mr. _" or "Dear Ms. _"
A mayor	"Dear Mayor _"
A councilmember	"Dear Councilmember _"
A bishop	"Dear Bishop _"
A priest	"Dear Father _"
A minister	"Dear Reverend _"
A rabbi	"Dear Rabbi _"
A king or queen	"Dear Sir or Madame" "May it please your Majesty"

If the salutation is	The complimentary close is
Dear (title and last name)	Sincerely, Yours truly, Very truly yours,
Dear (first name—familiar)	Sincerely, Cordially yours,
Dear (first name or nickname—very familiar)	Cordially, Best regards,

8.2.9 The signature block

The *signature block* is four spaces below the complimentary close and flush against the left margin. It contains the name of the writer and, on the next line, the title, office, or division of the writer.

8.2.10 The initials

The *initials* of the writer, or dictator, as well as those of the typist are often included two spaces below the close. As in the memo, the initials of the person writing are in capital letters and the typist's initials are in lower case letters.

8.2.11 The enclosure notation

The *enclosure notation* is located two spaces below the complimentary close or the initials and flush with the left margin. It may be abbreviated "Enc." If there is

8.3.1

more than one enclosure, "Enc." is followed by a numeral in parentheses indicating the number of enclosures. Titles of enclosures may be used when there are many enclosures to identify those that need to be signed by the reader.

8.2.12 The copy designation and second page heading

The *copy designation* and the *second page heading* are prepared like those of memos.

8.3

THE REPORT FORMAT

When a short report (one to three pages) is sent in-house, it follows the memo format. Short reports sent outside the organization generally use the letter format.

The long report (four or more pages) usually provides extensive research and, therefore, calls for more specialized formatting. The formal report is divided into three sections: the Preliminary Matter, the Discussion Matter, and the Back Matter. A sample report is found on page 133.

8.3.1 The preliminary matter

The preliminary matter may consist of the following components:

The *cover page* announces the identifying information to the reader.

The typeface on the cover should be larger and bolder than that used for the text.

The title of the report should be in capital letters (caps) and centered two to three inches or about 13 lines from the top of the page.

The name/s of the author/s and the date should be centered in the middle of the page.

The name of the company or department from which the report has been generated should be one inch from the bottom of the cover page.

The *letter of transmittal*, as the name implies, transmits the report and refers to the authorization or reason the report has been written. It might also highlight important points in the report, provide a summary of conclusions or recommendations, discuss side issues important to the reader, refer to any particular limits on the information presented, or acknowledge help given by others in the report preparation. It should be limited to one page. The letter of transmittal follows the regular letter format previously described.

The *title page* may repeat the same elements that appear on the cover page. While this page is counted as a small Roman numeral i, there is no number printed.

The *table of contents* lists the contents of the report.

The title of this page (typed: TABLE OF CONTENTS) should be in caps and centered about 13 lines from the top of the page.

The first entry should be about three lines from the title.

The headings and their corresponding page numbers should be close enough for ease of reading.

Each heading is double-spaced.

This page is counted as small Roman numeral ii,

8.3.1

and the number is centered about seven lines from the bottom of the page.

The *list of illustrations* includes all illustrations, tables, and graphs presented in the report.

The title (typed: ILLUSTRATIONS) should be in caps and centered about 13 lines from the top of the page.

The first entry should be about three lines from the title.

The name of each illustration and its corresponding page number should be close enough for ease of reading.

Each illustration heading is double-spaced.

This page is counted as small Roman numeral iii and the number is centered seven lines from the bottom of the page.

The *executive summary* is a brief synopsis of the entire report and stresses conclusions and recommendations. The executive summary is more effective if it is contained within one page.

The title (typed: EXECUTIVE SUMMARY) should be in caps and centered about 13 lines from the top of the page.

The text starts about three lines from the title and should be single-spaced.

This page is counted as a small Roman numeral iv and the number is centered about seven lines from the bottom of the page.

8.3.2 The discussion matter

The discussion matter may consist of four components: the introduction, graphics, conclusion, and the recommendation. The *introduction* lets the reader know what the report is about.

The descriptive title (typed: SECURITY AT RASCALS, INC.) should be in caps and centered on line 13 from the top of the page.

The text starts three lines from the title and should be double-spaced.

The page is counted as page 1 but the number is not printed.

The *discussion* is the body of the report.

If used, a chapter heading (typed: CHAPTER I) should be in caps and centered about 13 lines from the top of the page.

If the title of the chapter is short, include it on the same line as the chapter heading. If the title of the chapter is long, allow two lines and separate the title at natural phrase breaks, using single-space.

The running text of the discussion begins on the third line after the title.

The running text should be double-spaced and, after the first page, typed about two inches from the top of the page, one inch from the bottom, and one inch from the sides.

If *subheadings* (caps and lower case) are used in the running text, they can be centered, placed at the left margin, or used to begin paragraphs. Whatever method is chosen, remember to keep the format consistent as to spacing, underlining, and caps.

Paragraphs are separated by two spaces if block

8.3.2

form (no indentation) is used. Use a single space between paragraphs if indenting.

If a *quotation* is longer than three typed lines, skip a line, indent five spaces from either side of the margin, and single-space the quote. Then, skip another line, and continue with the running text. (Some academic writing now recommends double-spacing for long, set-off quotes, but this practice has not been adopted in most business writing.)

For items in a *list,* indent five spaces from each side margin and type the list single-spaced with one blank line above and below each list. If an item continues on a second line, align the turnover with the first word on the line above.

Graphics may also be inserted in both the formal and informal report. "Graphics" refers to tables and figures. Tables include randomly incorporated data, continuation tables, and formal tables. All other graphics are referred to as figures: bar charts, line graphs, circle graphs, flow charts, organization charts, drawings, maps, and photographs.

Insert graphics as close to their reference as possible rather than attached on separate pages.

Number and title tables *above* the data. Number and title figures *below* the graphic. The numbers and titles may be centered or placed flush against the left margin of the report.

If more than one table or figure is used in a report, number each in order of its appearance. Use Arabic numbers:

Table 1   Table 2   Table 3

Figure 1   Figure 2

If the report contains numbered chapters, use a decimal numbering system to indicate both the chapter and the number of the graphic:

Table 1.1   Table 1.2

Figure 1.1   Figure 1.2

Include a precise noun-phrase title with each graphic:

Table 1 Cost comparison of employee development programs

Table 2 Characteristics of Mynah Birds

FIGURE 1 SMOKE DETECTOR LOCATIONS

You may capitalize the first letter of the title, the first letters of each word in the title (except for articles, conjunctions, and prepositions), or all letters in the title. Use one method consistently throughout the report.

Single space titles that require more than one line. Consecutive lines are aligned under the first word of the title, not under the word "Table" or "Figure."

Graphics and titles should fit within the margins of the report.

When tables require more than one full page, begin the second page with the designation, the number, and the word "Continued":

Table 1 Continued

Explanatory notes, keys, and legends usually appear within the graphic itself or beneath the graphic in the left-hand position but above the number and title.

If graphics are borrowed, identify your source in parentheses after the title:

Table 1 Sample evaluation form (Courtesy of Human Resources Department, City and County of San Francisco)

Figure 1 Average Expenses per Department (Source: Craig E. Monet, *Where Is Your Money Going?* [Chicago: Gold Press, 1988], p. 20)

The *conclusion* ties everything together for the reader in the form of a summary.

The conclusion can be part of the running text or typed on a new page. If printed on a new page, the title (typed: CONCLUSION) should be in caps and centered about two inches or 13 lines from the top of the page.

The text starts about three lines from the centered title and should be double-spaced.

The *recommendations* propose what should be done based on the findings of the report. If this section is included, follow the same format as that used for the conclusion.

8.3.3 The back matter

The *back matter* may consist of three components.

The *glossary,* if necessary, provides brief definitions for specialized vocabulary.

The title (typed: GLOSSARY) should be in caps and centered about two inches or 13 lines from the top of the page.

The first key term and explanation starts about

three lines from the title and falls within the one-inch side margins.

The key term is bold faced, caps and lower case, followed by a period, two spaces, and the explanation.

The bottom margin of this section is one inch from the bottom of the page.

The *appendices* contain additional information relevant to the text but excluded from the text because it would interfere with readability or because it is too bulky. The appendices might include documents such as a chart of raw survey data used in the report, historical background, or the full text of another relevant report.

The title (typed: APPENDIX) should be in caps and centered about two inches or 13 lines from the top of the page.

Each item or document included is placed in a separate appendix and is lettered successively. (Appendix A, Appendix B, and to the end of the alphabet, if necessary. If, heaven forbid, you have more than 26 appendices, double the letters of the alphabet [Appendix AA, Appendix BB].)

The bottom margin of this section is one inch from the bottom of the page.

Notes serve two purposes: They provide comments on the running text and identify the source of the quoted material. They may appear in the running text or at the end of the report. Most word processing programs have a footnote function, but, if yours does not or if you are preparing your report on a typewriter, use the following guidelines.

Comments are at the bottom of the page. Indent five spaces, key in the corresponding number in the text, place a period, add two spaces, and comment.

If a comment continues on the second line, align the turnover with the first word in the line above.

The last line should be one inch from the bottom of the page.

Footnotes are at the bottom of the page. Indent five spaces, key in the corresponding number in the text, place a period, add two spaces, and include the following information: author's first and last names, title of the source (underlined or in italics if it is a book; surrounded by quotation marks if it is a magazine article or report), publisher, year, and page.

If a note continues on the second line, align the turnover with the first word in the line above. The last line should be one inch from the bottom of the page.

Endnotes are on their own page, after the appendices. The title (typed: ENDNOTES) should be in caps and centered on about line 13 from the top of the page.

The first entry starts three lines below the title. The endnote information is typed in the same manner as the footnotes.

Number each endnote flush with the side margin. If an item continues on the second line, align the turnover with the first word in the line above.

Single space endnotes and leave double spaces between them.

The last line should be one inch from the bottom of the page.

Textnotes are in parentheses as part of the text. The same ordering of reference information for footnotes and endnotes is used.

SAMPLE REPORT

Title
page

COMMUNICATION AND HUGS:
ATTRITION AT C&R

Prepared for
the Department of Human Resources
b y

Michael J. Fretwell, Convener
Human Resources

Lois E. Mendlesohn
Floor Operations

Walter E. Benson
Supply

Lee M. Moore
Bookkeeping Services

Rex R. Broodman
Accounts Receivable

Carmen R. Santiago
Office Support

Jack H. Hewlitt
Planning

Miriam S. Sinapolis
Delivery

C&R MANUFACTURING, INC.
July 19, 19__

**Executive
summary**   **EXECUTIVE SUMMARY**

The following report discusses the conclusions of the special
committee on employee attrition. It finds three main causes for the
large attrition rates of March, April, and May of this year: 1) the
various stresses caused by the relocation of the company's main
plant, 2) a perceived decrease in company benefits, and 3) rumors
generated by the recent management reorganization. Overall, these
were symptomatic of what we believe to be a temporary disregard
for employee communication brought on by the relocation. To
ensure that such a problem does not happen again, the report makes
two recommendations for action by the Department of Human
Resources.

COMMUNICATION AND SECURITY: ATTRITION AT C&R

I. BACKGROUND INFORMATION

C&R Manufacturing has played an important role in the development of the Midway community since the company's founding in 1892. Not only has C&R provided a consistent source of tax revenue and contributed to the growth of other support industries, it has also paid wages to a large portion of Midway's population. Last year, for example, the company employed over 1000 members of the Midway community. C&R has prided itself on providing stable employment for the community and has been repaid by a stable commitment on the part of its employees.

During March, April, and May of this year, however, there was a large number of resignations from the company. Twenty–five of the 194 were the planned result of the recent management buyout. But 167 were not. This is almost one fifth of the workforce and has been very disturbing news for a company for which turnover has been traditionally low.

exodus. This report fulfills that function. Prepared under the direction of the Department of Human Resources, it is the result of a study completed by a company–wide committee which analyzed employee exit interviews (See Appendix One for mandate). This committee, chaired by a representative from Human Resources, comprised two representatives from management, two from the white collar segment, and three from blue collar employees. The employee union was not represented though it was asked and its input and advice were solicited.

Essentially, the committee read the summaries of all exit interviews conducted over the past six months to determine the primary reasons for the high employee attrition rate. When necessary, the committee consulted with experts inside and outside the company. As you will see in reading the report, a single reason was not found, but three important factors came into play: the relocation of the company's main plant, the decrease in company benefits, and the recent management reorganization.

II. THREE REASONS FOR EMPLOYEE ATTRITION

A.   The Plant Relocation

Employee exit interviews indicate that the largest number of resignations (107) came about because of the move from the Richard Street to the Plum Road site.

The Richard Street site was synonymous with C&R for most of the company's history. Because C&R's work has never involved heavy industry, the neighborhood around the Richard Street plant has always been residential. As a result, many of our employees lived very close, sometimes within walking distance of the plant.

Also, because so many (a recent survey suggested nearly 62 percent) of the employees lived near the plant, the surrounding community had developed a support system. Nearby stores and eating establishments posted company notices and provided an unofficial message and job finder's network. Children were picked up after school by neighborhood members and taken to the local park where they were enrolled in convenient after–school programs. The services of the programs themselves were often formed around the needs of company workers.

Several years ago, Dr. Ichabod Standhoff completed a dissertation that analyzed this close identification of the employees with the Richard Street site (*Community   Company/Company Community: An Analysis of the Role of One Company in the Life of a Community*, Department of Industrial Psychology, State University, Midway, 19—). According to Dr. Standhoff, many employees saw C&R as more than just a worksite; it had become an essential part of their lives. In a recent interview conducted in conjunction with our committee's work, Dr. Standhoff suggested that moving the plant outside the community could have created three reactions[1]:

Text note

1.   What was once a simple walk to work now became a "commute." Even though this "commute" was less than 22

Footnote

---

[1]The committee and Dr. Standhoff would like to stress that his comments are simply hypotheses. A follow–up study would need to be completed to prove or disprove these suggestions. The committee includes them here because a majority found them interesting enough for inclusion and because it was obvious that they reflected much of the committee's thinking.

miles, the *idea* of commuting could have become so strong that workers would want to work elsewhere.

2.   Moving the plant also affected the support system used by many employees. This was particularly important for female employees who are primary family caregivers. As primary caregivers, they sought employment closer to the base of their families. (In fact, a significant percentage of women leaving the company [46%] cited this reason.)

3.   Hypothesis one and two coupled with the actual move created a major change. As a reaction to change, many employees became alienated and addressed this alienation by leaving the company. In effect, said Dr. Standhoff, leaving the company was a way of punishing C&R for forcing the change upon them.

Subheading
B.   "Reduced" Employee Benefits

Shortly after the moved–based resignations, C&R experienced a second wave of employee resignations. All of these (a surprisingly high number of 27) left, they said, because employee benefits were cut. One employee summarized the reports of several when he commented:

I'm leaving because, as I figure it, if you add together the small pay increase we received this year, the increased cost of commuting, and the decrease in employee benefits, my compensation has been cut 30% this year. And the cost of living went up 20%.

Several other employees made similar comments, but the actual process by which the 30% figure was determined was never clearly stated in the interviews. We assumed that the "benefit cut" mentioned so frequently was the decrease in the employer's contribution that was negotiated in the employee contract. We also assumed that the "30%" figure was the result of employee gossip and that the company, caught up in the logistics and problems caused by the recent move, had not corrected the gossip.

Moreover, we also assumed that, though this decrease in the employer contribution was negotiated prior to the move to Plum Road, it became increasingly more important to employees after the move. This would seem to be borne out by the vehemence—and expletives—expressed in the comments.

C.   Management Reorganization

Finally, the recent senior management reorganization caused a ripple effect throughout the company which increased employee insecurity.

As far as we could tell, there was not much employee bitterness felt by managers whose jobs were consolidated or abolished. The interviews with the 25 managers eliminated indicated they were relatively happy with the company buyout, and the 15 who did not retire early appreciated the company's effort to help them find new jobs.

Middle management, however, seemed to fear that its jobs would be cut next. Thirteen managers, in fact, stated that they were leaving because they feared that senior management downsizing was a first wave of other cuts yet to come. Since, as far as we know, no such downsizing is planned, this was undoubtedly the result of another rumor. In fact, the notes of the Human Resource notetakers contain six references to gossip as the source of the downsizing rumors. Dr. Standhoff told us that the gossip itself could be related to employee alienation.[2]

Moreover, we also found that a surprising number (23) of non–management employees left because they felt that the present downsizing would cut off possibilities of promotion. These were well–trained, white collar workers, most of whom (16) said that they had originally come to the company because of the possibilities for promotion.

III.   CONCLUSION

These, then—the various stresses caused by the relocation of the company's main plant, the perceived decrease in company benefits, and the rumors generated by the recent management reorganization—can be listed as the specific causes for last spring's huge departure. The mandate of this committee asked for no more than this list, but the Committee felt that the evidence suggested at least two general conclusions that the Company might wish to heed.

Footnote

---

[2]See previous note

1.   The idea of moving sites caused a communication rift between managers and employees. ⹁Management was so concerned with the logistics of the move that it did not pause to consider the emotional needs of the employees. It is easy to see how this happened; after all, C&R had been on the Richard Street site for over 100 years. To management, the logistical magnitude of such a move seemed to dominate every thought. On the other hand, it is also easy to see that the emotional stress of the move was compounded for many employees by the apparent lack of management concern and information about the effects of the move.

2.   In the absence of a clear information line, gossip became the dominant information source. This meant many distortions and fabrications were treated as fact by employees.

IV.   RECOMMENDATIONS

We would assume that what happened at C&R was a one–time situation. However, we think it important for all employees of the company that we guard against the possibility of a future occurrence. As a result, we would like to make two suggestions.

1.   The company should begin a weekly newsletter, the main goal of which would be to present accurate, complete information. Daily information might even be presented

on video. Another networking line should be included
that would answer employee questions quickly and
accurately.

2. The company should also tap into the gossip lines. The
    committee briefly looked into the Core Group concept as
    one example of such tapping. In Core Groups, individuals
    are used within the company to collect rumor and report
    it to the information service and to dispense corrective
    information when necessary. Because the Core Group
    leader is an officially identified source within the
    company, employees will go to this person to find out
    answers or to pass on information.

We feel that these two simple steps, well executed, would
result in better communication and employee morale.
Communication is the key to improved employee morale—
communication, that is, and a warm hug now and then.

APPENDIX ONE

C&R
MEMO   June 6, 19__

        TO: Michael J. Fretwell
                    Human Resources

      FROM: Rosa R. Begum, Director
                    Human Resources

SUBJECT: Special Committee on Employee Resignations

As you know, C&R has experienced a very high number of resignations during the past months. Naturally, this coupled with the move to the Plum Street site has caused a great deal of stress within the company. Several of our managers and the stockholders have asked questions about these resignations, and Human Resources has not been able to respond adequately because there has not been a thorough study. I would like you to convene a committee to complete that study.

The members of the committee represent a cross section of the company: two members each from management and the white collar sector and three from the blue collar segment. You might also ask for union representation if the union would like to be involved.

We wouldn't want to limit the committee in any way, but I would suggest that you consult the exit interviews Human Resources has conducted with all employees who have left the company. Please feel free to use any other information inside or outside the company which you might think relevant.

I will notify the other members of the committee that you will be calling them. I will also ask them to send you their schedules of availability. Please deliver the report to me by the end of July.

Fretwell
Page 2.

I will notify the other members of the committee that you will be calling them. I will also ask them to send you their schedules of availability. Please deliver the report to me by the end of July.

Remember to call on me whenever I can be of help.

cc: Walter E. Benson
       Rex R. Broodman
       Jack H. Hewlitt
       Lois E. Mendlesohn
       Lee M. Moore
       Carmen R. Santiago
       Miriam S. Sinapolis

Proofreading Carefully

Proofreading is the most thankless task in the writing process. If you do it well, no one will ever comment on your work. If you do it poorly, readers will accuse you of carelessness.

Moreover, proofreading is not fun. There are few things more tedious than poring over a text, particularly one you have written yourself, looking for errors. No wonder so many writers try to avoid it!

But good proofreading is essential to the overall success of your document, whether it be a letter, memo, or report. While attention to detail may be an innate trait, anyone can improve proofreading skills. Improvement is simply a matter of following the simple steps in the process.

9.1

BE PHYSICALLY AND MENTALLY PREPARED

Physically and mentally preparing yourself for the task is one of the keys to successful proofreading.

Know Your Proofreading Responsibilities

When you are proofreading your own work, anything goes. Change, twist, rearrange, and shout over the document all you want. When reading another's document, you should be more careful of the writer's feelings. Find out specifically what is expected of you. Does the writer want you to change the substance of the text, simply root out the mechanical errors, or discuss every change? Knowing what is expected of you before you begin can save you a great deal of grief later.

9.1.1 Prepare your workspace

9.1.2

Several simple techniques can improve the physical environment of your proofreading space and, therefore, increase your proofreading accuracy.

Work in a quiet place. While you might not be able to proofread in a sound-proof room, you should find a place that is reasonably quiet. Choose a time of day when work is slowest and choose a place that is as far as possible from the hustle and bustle of work.

Use a table and comfortable chair. You can't proofread on the run. Sit down at a table and in a comfortable chair to complete your proofreading duties. The table allows you to concentrate on the work at hand, and the comfortable chair keeps your mind off the aches and pains of a weary body.

Gather all of your support materials. Before you begin, place your pencils, rulers, dictionary, and grammar handbook on the table. It wastes time and breaks your concentration whenever you must leave the proofreading space to look around for support materials that should be at hand.

9.1.2 Clear your mind

Not only should you physically prepare yourself to proofread but you should also mentally prepare yourself.

Plan your time. Determine how much time it will take you to proofread the document, and schedule regular breaks. If you don't proofread much, you will find that 15 minutes is about the maximum amount of time that you can sustain your concentration when you are working alone. Don't try to push yourself much further. Take a short three- to five-minute

9.2

"Can You Take a Moment to Look at This?"

Don't give in to the temptation to read something on the fly! You are never an accurate proofreader when you are in a hurry. Always demand at least 15 quiet minutes before looking at something for anyone else. If proofreading your own work, schedule at least a 15-minute break from the actual writing—24 hours is better—before editing and proofreading.

---

break before returning to the task. If you are working with another person, your working period can be extended.

Stay interested. It is easy to say, "Stay interested"; it is often more difficult to carry out the rule. This is a question of putting your mind over the matter at hand. Convince yourself that you *will* do a good job and remind yourself that careless proofreading is generally the result of inattention.

Scan the document. Before you begin to read, scan the document so that you have a general idea of its purpose and scope. Also, if you are proofreading for another person, check to see if there are any instructions from the author.

9.2

READ SLOWLY

Most poor proofreading is done too quickly. Read very slowly, one or two words at a time, and read

9.3

line by line rather than for the sweep of the document. There are two techniques to follow that will force you to slow down.

9.2.1 One-person reading

Use a short, nontransparent ruler to reveal each line of type and move slowly down the page. As you move the ruler down the page line by line, focus on one or two words at a time and never more than a line at a time. If you are correcting on a computer screen, use a plastic ruler to run down the screen or bring up the type one line at a time.

If you have a "perfect" copy and a copy to proofread, use the same technique but use a ruler on each copy as you compare texts.

9.2.2 Two-person comparison reading

If the document is over three pages long, an efficient and effective way of proofreading is for two people to read it together. Using a ruler to reveal each line, the reader should read slowly and clearly, articulating every syllable. Foreign or difficult words should be spelled out. The reader should also note aloud the punctuation, the capitalization, and the format such as indentations and spacing. The second person marks the text for corrections. Both proofers are looking for errors.

9.3

READ METHODICALLY

Good proofreading generally involves reading the document at least three times. The first time, read for content and organization, the second for mechanical

9.3.1

To Print or Not to Print

It is convenient to work with paper or hard copy when proofreading, but many companies prefer that proofreading be completed before printing the material. All of the techniques used here can be adapted to screen reading if you use a nontransparent plastic ruler or you bring up the text one line at a time. If you are proofing from the screen, schedule more frequent breaks—1 minute for every 10 minutes of proofing, for example—to relieve eyestrain.

---

errors, the third for formatting problems. Reading systematically three times forces you to focus on just one type of problem at a time.

9.3.1 Look for errors in content and organization

A good technique to use when proofreading is to cast yourself into the role of the targeted reader. Try to read the document as you imagine this reader would. In doing so, ask yourself the key questions about content.

Is the objective clear early in the document?

Has the document achieved its objective? Would you do what it wants you to do? If not, why not?

Is the document complete? Can you read it without having to ask questions?

Is the text logical? Do you find yourself wondering how the writer arrived at a particular conclusion?

Check the Front with the Back

In a long report, check the titles, subtitles, graphics, and page numbers against the table of contents.

Is the tone correct? Is it friendly? Does the style talk *with* you, not *at* you or *down* to you?

9.3.2 Look for the most common mechanical errors

Mechanical errors are errors in the text. They include grammar and typographical errors. As Chapter 4 points out, the following are among the most common grammar errors:

Incomplete and run-on sentences

Nonagreement of subject and verb

Unclear pronoun reference or disagreement of pronoun and referent

Incorrect parallel structure

Dangling or misplaced modifiers

The most common typographical errors include the following:

Incorrect capitalization

Incorrect dates

Incorrect or deleted punctuation

Incorrect spelling of names

9.3.3

> ### Look for Nests of Errors
> When you find an error, watch for a nest of other errors nearby. Writers and typesetters have a habit of losing their concentration in spurts.

Insertion of an extra letter or letters
Misspelled words
Omission of words or parts of words
Repeated words or phrases
Reversed letters
Reversed numbers

9.3.3 Check for formatting consistency

There is no perfect way to format a report. (See Chapter 8 for possibilities.) Any format will work as long as you are consistent. To achieve this consistency, use a style sheet.

A style sheet is a document that lists the important formatting rules for the documents you create. If everyone in your office uses the same style sheet, every letter that leaves the office or company will have the same format. Making a style sheet just for your own use can also save you much time in your final read through of the document.

Make sure that your style sheet contains notes on the following points:

Abbreviations, acronyms, and *initializations.* They should be consistent throughout.

Bibliographies, graphics, and *footnotes.* In a long report, particularly, check that the information in the table of contents, index, and bibliography is in the correct and consistent order.

Capitalization and *spelling*. Again, consistency and correctness are the only matters here.

Dates. Is it April 1, 2000; 4/1/00; or 1 April 2000? Be consistent throughout your writing.

Margins. Review the spacing and margins.

Headings. Make sure that your headings are consistent throughout the document. Your main points should have one style and your subpoints another. What typeface are you using?

Hyphens. If it is "life-long" in one sentence, it shouldn't be "lifelong" in the next. Check a dictionary for the preferred usage.

Numerals. Which numbers are spelled out and which are used in their Arabic form?

Any other special problems you might want to include.

9.3.3

C&R (no spaces)	Use footnotes (10pt New York font) to explain Use in-text notes for references Text is in 12 pt. New York type	Brody. Santiago Sinapolis
Abbreviations, Acronyms, and Initializations	**Bibliographies, Graphics, and Footnotes**	**Capitalization and Spelling**
	Indent paragraphs Indent lists 5 (for bullets or numbers) Indent text for lists 10	Title page 24 pt N.Y. and/or all caps First page title 14 pt N.Y. all caps bold face. First level headings 14 pt b.f. all caps Centered Second level 12 pt b.f. CLC — Flush left
Dates	**Margins**	**Headings**
	1–9 spell out First level head Roman numerals Second level heads. (letters A/B/C.	
Hyphenation	**Numerals**	**Special Problems or Concerns**

Preparing Your Personal Writing Program

10.1

Even very good writers are called upon to change their writing. Some might be working in a new field. Others have a new boss. Still others find that they must change their writing to communicate with a new audience. Likewise, it is not unusual for a student writer at the top in English literature to struggle through papers in marketing or pre-law. All of these cases are not only usual, they are natural.

Every field, every profession, every job, and every company will make new demands on the writer. With these changing demands, the careful writer will learn to adapt. However, it is important to remember two things: this adaptation does not necessarily mean improvement and having to change your writing does *not* mean you are a bad writer.

It takes the average writer about two and a half years to become comfortable with writing on the job. This seems like a long time, but when you consider the changes that a writer or a company can go through in two and a half years—one of our clients once told us about having six supervisors during a two-year period—the figure seems more than reasonable. There are, however, methods by which you can shorten that learning time. One of the best ways is to develop a personal writing program.

A personal writing program is a list showing what you must change in your writing. If you have a teacher or supervisor who is supportive, we suggest that you share your finished writing program with him or her. Better yet, if you can work out your writing program with your instructor or supervisor, you can begin your program even faster. No matter how you devise your list, once you have begun, stick to it. Writing doesn't change overnight, but your writing will get better with each document you compose.

Use the following process to develop your writing program:

1. Prepare yourself mentally to change your writing.

2. Decide what needs to be changed in your writing and what strategies you will use to make the changes.

3. List the facets of your writing you want to change in order of priority.

What follows are some of the more common problem areas for writers and some of the strategies you can use to make changes in these areas.

10.1

PREPARE YOURSELF MENTALLY TO CHANGE YOUR WRITING

Most of us develop a fond attachment to the words we string together. As a result, it is often harder to overlook our emotional investment in our own words than it is to learn to adapt. Moreover, many times the changes we must make are not a case of right or wrong. These changes are simply a question of adapting our writing to a new audience.

In preparing a writing program, try to forget this emotional investment and concentrate on figuring out what the editor is telling you. If you have a supervisor or teacher who likes to mark up things, consider yourself lucky. Look at each of those red marks as an opportunity to learn. If your editor does not mark your document, be sure you understand what you are being told. Repeat the problem back to your editor just to make sure that both of you are working on the same wave length.

10.2

DECIDE WHAT NEEDS TO BE CHANGED IN YOUR WRITING AND WHAT STRATEGIES YOU WILL USE TO MAKE THE CHANGES

Look through several samples of your writing and note each of the comments made by your editor. Try to classify these comments into general categories such as "unclear pronoun reference" or "repetition of vocabulary." Then, try to consolidate your list into larger groupings. We use four categories when we work with our clients: *Content, Organization, Mechanics,* and *Style.* What follows are some easy-to-apply strategies we suggest for making changes in each.

10.2.1 Make changes to the content

Any writing program should start with the content. If you aren't getting the content right, it seems a waste of time to try to correct the document. There are several ways to eliminate repeated problems in the content of writing.

10.2.1.1 Understand the assignment. Begin by making sure that you understand the assignment. It is not uncommon for a new writer to have a document returned with comments saying the point of the assignment has been missed. If this happens more than once, however, you have a problem. You and your editor are not understanding each other. Sometimes you are not listening carefully; sometimes editors don't know what they actually want until they see the work.

The easiest way to correct this problem is, as we have said in Chapter 3, to put the assignment into writing. Putting the assignment in writing is a good place to start focusing. A good written assignment will include the specific subject, the purpose, the reader or audience, the required length, and, if necessary, the format and due date.

10.2.1

EXAMPLE:

I will prepare a one- to two-page report justifying two new Clerical Staff IV positions in our department. The new hires will be used to process Disposition and Review Reports. I will indicate why the two positions are necessary and what their responsibilities will include. The report will be completed by Wednesday, June 24, so that it can be on the Personnel Director's desk by Friday, June 26.

EXAMPLE:

I will create and write down the questions for a questionnaire that customers can use to audit energy use at home. The questionnaire will be no longer than two pages. I will have the draft completed in two weeks.

A clear written assignment will save you time in the long run and get you focused on the assignment.

10.2.1.2 Learn to eliminate information. If your document comes back from the editor with large sections crossed out, or if you continually write letters and memos of more than one page, you are probably guilty of overkill. The solution to this problem is to cut. The problem for most writers is what to cut.

To eliminate an overabundance of ideas, review the purpose statement of your writing. Then, look at each sentence and determine how much of the information supports or fits your purpose. If the reader can live without the idea, draw a line through it. Forget what the writing "sounds" like. When you finish this exercise, you should have only a few sentences or fragments of sentences. This is the "meat" of your communication.

10.2.1

Rewrite now, placing the most important idea, the purpose statement, at the beginning of the document. After you have completed this exercise a few times, you will find that the amount you are cutting will decrease. You will naturally edit your work as you write the draft.

10.2.1.3 Include *all* of the essential details. Not including enough information is a harder problem to recognize. After all, if you didn't think you had included enough, you would have included more. However, if you find that your work comes back often with suggestions for more information, this may be your problem.

Practice role playing to deal with this problem. Put aside your document for at least an hour. When you pick it up again, read it critically as if you were the intended audience. Ask yourself the key questions, "As the reader, would I be persuaded to do what this docu-

---

A Checklist for Content

1. Focus on the purpose statement.

   (a) Is there a purpose statement in the opening lines of the writing?

   (b) Does the statement present an accurate introduction to the content?

2. Review the content.

   (a) Does the data logically lead to the conclusions?

   (b) Are all of the details relevant to the purpose and conclusion?

   (c) Is there adequate detail or explanation to support the purpose statement?

ment wants me to do? Is there enough information to decide? Is there enough information for me to respond easily? Do I feel satisfied with the message?" Revise your work based on your answers.

Finally, before turning in your work, review it using "A Checklist for Content" (page 160).

10.2.2 Make changes in the organization

People rarely tell you that your work is poorly organized. If they are kind, they will say it "doesn't flow." If they are more blunt, they will tell you that it "jumps around a lot" or "doesn't make sense."

Poor organization generally comes about because the writer has tried to string ideas together while writing. Outlining is the answer to this problem. An outline in this case is not necessarily a formal, typed outline with Roman numerals and capital letters. A few notes scratched on note paper or a few lines typed into the word processor are sufficient in most cases.

If the document is a relatively short letter or memo, use the outlines suggested in Chapter 2. Simply place your ideas in the order suggested; then, write your sentences to connect them.

If the document is longer, outline as we suggested in Chapter 3. In this case, begin with a list of main ideas—in full sentences, if possible. Your organization will be even stronger if, under these ideas, you can include the topic sentences needed to support your ideas.

Once your list is made, arrange it in an appropriate order. Chapter 3 makes several suggestions for patterns.

Finally, before submitting the document, review it using "A Checklist for Organization" (page 162).

10.2.2

A Checklist for Organization

1. Focus on the purpose statement.
   (a) Is the purpose statement clear?
   (b) Does it present an accurate overview of the content?
   (c) Does it indicate a direct or indirect format?
2. Review the accuracy of the report's divisions.
   (a) Are there an introduction, body, and conclusion?
   (b) Are the points in the body of equal length and/or importance?
   (c) Are the sections distinct from each other?
3. Present ideas in the most effective organizational pattern.
   (a) Is the "good news" or informative message presented using a direct format?
   (b) Is the "bad news" or persuasive message presented using the indirect format?
4. Review the flow of the writing in the body of the report.
   (a) If the writing is a narrative, are the ideas in chronological order?
   (b) If the writing describes a place, object, or structure, are the details in spatial order?
   (c) If the writing is topical, are the ideas presented in an effective logical order (e.g., general to specific, specific to general, most agreeable to least agreeable, least important to most important)?
5. Review the clarity of transitions between sentences and paragraphs.

A WRITER IN NEED OF A PERSONAL WRITING PROGRAM (EMPHASIZING CONTENT AND ORGANIZATION)

10.2.2

TO: James Mather
             Accounts Manager

FROM: Marshall Lee
             Data Processing Support

SUBJECT: Changing Data Base
             Column Widths

I have passed on your comments about Janet Lowell to her, and she would like me to include her "thanks" with this memo. We really appreciate your support. It is our job to provide whatever service we can, but we appreciate comments that say our service is appreciated.

Least important idea at the beginning

In your memo, you asked me if you could widen or decrease the width of the columns on the data base display and on the printer. If information in one category is too wide for the current column width, you can widen the column. If the information is narrower than the column width, the width can be decreased. So, you can increase or decrease the width of the columns.

Irrelevant information

Main idea buried

Increasing or decreasing the column width helps you make the report look exactly the way you want it and shows the information most effectively. It also ensures that the information fits correctly on the printer.

More irrelevancy

WRITING REVISED

10.2.2

TO: James Mather
            Accounts Manager

FROM: Marshall Lee
            Data Processing Support

SUBJECT: Changing Data Base
            Column Widths

You can increase or decrease the width of the columns on both the display screen and the printer. To increase the current column width, place the cursor at the right limit of the column and press "Control W" ("Ctrl W"). The column will widen one space. Repeat pressing "Ctrl W" until the column is at the width you need.

Main idea placed at the beginning

First idea explained

When the information is narrower than the column width, place the cursor at the right column limit. Press "Ctrl N" until the margin is as narrow as you need.

Second idea explained

I'd like you to know that I have passed on your praise of Janet Lowell to her, and she would like me to include her "thanks" with this memo. While we realize that our job is to provide service, it is nice to know that our service is appreciated. A copy of your note will go into Ms. Lowell's personnel file.

Least important idea included

Call me at 543-7711 whenever you would like my help.

10.2.3 Improve mechanics

Because there is a right or wrong about most mechanical problems, mechanics is the easiest thing to improve. Mechanics means formatting, spelling, punctuation, and grammar. The first two areas have special correction strategies; the second two involve a little more concentration and effort.

10.2.3.1 Use a consistent format. There is no excuse for formatting errors, but, nonetheless, most of us make them. Because formatting is a question of memory, the simplest solution for formatting errors is a style sheet such as the one we suggested in Chapter 9. Make a style sheet for each of the formats you use. Keep it near your work station and review it before you begin a document. You will soon find that you have memorized the information, and formatting will come naturally to you. When you start a new job or change jobs within a company, make sure that you make a new style sheet for your documents.

10.2.3.2. Improve your spelling. It is comforting to know, given the large number of poor spellers writing today, that spelling has little to do with intelligence. Some scientists attribute one's ability to spell to genetic encoding—you inherit your spelling ability. Better news is that because spelling is a matter of visual and mental dexterity, just as you can learn to catch a ball, you can improve your spelling.

If you are a spelling weakling, there are several books or parts of books that outline how to improve your spelling. Improvement takes time and concentration, but if spelling is a serious problem, these books can help you build your spelling strength.

Whether you feel that spelling is a major handicap to your writing or you realize that you are apt to make spelling mistakes, you should invest in a computer dictionary. Some of these even flag homonyms (words like "principle/principal" that sound alike but have different spellings and meanings). Given the efficiency of these programs, there should never be a spelling error in your writing.

10.2.3.3 Correct grammar and punctuation.

Grammar and punctuation usage are two of the aspects of your writing that are easiest to improve. This can be accomplished by focusing on one type of error at a time, learning to correct the error, and becoming so used to making the correction that you do it naturally.

Begin by finding the errors. As we have said before, if you are serious about developing your writing program, you will be doing this anyway. Look at the list of problems you have drawn from your sample writing. Make a new list of all the grammar and punctuation errors that have occurred in your writing. Include the number of times each error has occurred in the sample.

Right before you turn in your next document, review it one more time, concentrating only on the error with the highest number on the list. Assume that you have finished the following paragraphs and are going to check them for nonagreement of subject and verb:

> Most *people* <u>consider</u> grammar and punctuation to be the key elements in writing. Moreover, *they* <u>think</u> that *they* <u>have</u> writing trouble because *they* <u>can't</u> remember grammar or punctuation rules. Both *beliefs* <u>are</u> wrong.

> *It* <u>is</u> possible to write *something* that <u>has</u> poor grammar and punctuation and that still <u>communicates</u> to the reader with a certain power. There <u>are</u> also many excellent business *writers* who do the right thing without being able to remember a single grammatical rule.

The first paragraph is simple enough. "People" is plural and so is the verb. "They" is plural and so are the verbs. "Beliefs" is plural and so is the verb.

The second paragraph might be a little troublesome. The first sentence is easy. The singular "is" agrees with the pronoun "It." The second sentence might be more difficult, however. The subject of "has" might not be readily apparent; the verb agrees with the pronoun-subject "that" which stands for "something." "Something" is singular, so the verb is correct. Likewise, "communicates" agrees with "that" which stands for "something." "Are" might also be troublesome, but the agreement is correct because "are" agrees with "writers."

Work through the entire document in this way focusing only on the one problem. Most of the time you will be correct, but in discovering why you are right, you will also be learning to spot the problem. We find that when you do this three or four times, the problem disappears from the writing. Psychologists call this "internalizing"; you naturally correct the problem without thinking about it. Once that happens, move on to the next problem on your list. It might take a couple of months, but eventually you will work your way through the whole list, and the problems will have naturally disappeared.

Get Thee a Grammar Check!!

Computer grammar checks are not entirely the answer to improving grammar and punctuation. They don't catch all errors, and they seem to spend much time marking things that one might think are irrelevant to good communication. They do provide, however, excellent aid in proofreading and help increase the liveliness of writing. All those who write regularly should have one installed on their computer.

10.2.4

We have one important reminder about this technique. Don't try to focus on more than one problem at a time. It is almost impossible to concentrate when you have too many things in the air.

10.2.4 Adapt the style

Style is how we put words together. No two people phrase or style their ideas exactly alike. Each of us develops an internal voice by which we form language. This individual voice is why it is so difficult to adapt our style to new models.

Chapter 1 has made several relevant suggestions. Sentences should be short, active, and positive and written to express ideas rather than to impress the reader. However, even if you are familiar with these guidelines, you might still have trouble adapting your style to your editor's.

If your writing is returned with vague comments about "not saying it correctly" or "it sounds better like

---

Beware the "Tinkerer"

Some supervisors or editors are incapable of reading someone else's document without making some changes in it. We call these people "tinkerers." There is very little you can do about this personality type. Writers can try to explain to tinkerers how they feel at having their acceptable words changed, but most often the tinkerer will reply that the changes have made the document "better." If you are dealing with a tinkerer, the best thing to do is learn to accept this foible, and look at your work as a collaboration with the editor.

10.2.4

this," your style might be the problem. Assuming that the comments are valid, these are parts of your style that can be easily changed. The most common problems in the style area include faulty tone, incorrect emphasis, or unfamiliar phrasing.

10.2.4.1 Adjust the tone. Tone is the degree of formality in your writing. All ideas can be expressed in at least three levels of tone: Formal, Standard, and Informal English.

Formal: Your expeditious reply will be appreciated and will enable us to begin procurement of materials as soon as possible.

Standard: Your materials will be purchased as soon as we receive your purchase order.

Informal: Hey you guys! You ain't going to get anything until you send in a new p.o.

In most cases, Standard English is preferred.

Role playing is a good way to improve the tone in a piece of writing. When you are writing or revising your work, pretend that the reader is someone you don't know very well. This should give you a degree of naturalness without going overboard with familiarity.

10.2.4.2 Adjust the sentence emphasis. If your writing sounds repetitive or choppy, or if you are told the main ideas are not clearly stated, sentence emphasis is probably the problem. There is one major rule for sentence emphasis: combine ideas so that the main ideas are in the main parts of the sentence and the subordinate ideas are in the subordinate parts.

No: The bad weather delayed the shipment of parts. The repairer was unable to make the needed repairs. The press remained idle.

10.2.4

Yes: *The bad weather delayed the shipment of parts,* and *the repairer was unable to make the needed repairs,* so *the press remained idle.*

Yes: Because the bad weather delayed the shipment of parts, and the repairer was unable to make the needed repairs, *the press remained idle.*

All three examples are grammatically correct. The "No" example, however, is choppy, and it is not clear which item on the list is important. In the first "Yes" example, it is clear that each item in the series of events is important. In the second "Yes" example, the bad weather and repairer are reduced to causes for the main idea, the idle press.

To improve sentence emphasis and the general flow of your writing style, get a good sentence structure workbook—your nearest college bookstore should have one—and complete the examples on sentence combining. It can be a tedious job, but it can be invaluable.

10.2.4.3 Adjust the phrasing. Musicians learn that the phrasing of classical music is different from that of jazz. And jazz musicians must change their phrasing to play rock 'n roll. Phrasing in writing is the same. As we said earlier, professions, companies, and even individual offices will express themselves differently. Many factors, such as geography, product, and audience account for differences in phrasing. Because there are so many variables, business writers are continually called upon to adjust their written phrasing.

The easiest way to adapt phrasing is to copy somebody else's. Figure out who the good writers are and copy their style. Look at successful letters in the files, figure out why they are successful, and adapt those successful features into your own writing. Learning to write well often involves copying the best models available.

> ## Caution: Models May Be Hazardous to Your Writing Health
>
> We have just said that copying good models is an excellent way to improve writing style. All of this assumes that the models that are copied are good ones. Entire professions—academics, government service, law—have been infected by writers using gobbledygook as the standard. Make sure the model you copy is a good one. Remember, if it is difficult to read, the style is not a model for you.

10.3

10.3

LIST THE FACETS OF YOUR WRITING YOU WANT TO CHANGE IN ORDER OF PRIORITY

Once you have derived your notes from several documents, it is time to put them together into a writing program. If you are lucky enough to find that all of the problem areas fall into one category, make a simple list.

My Personal Writing Program

1. Nonagreement of subject and verb

2. Unclear pronoun reference

3. Misplaced modifier

Before you turn in your next document, read it once, focusing only on the first thing on the list. After a few times of this concentrated focus, the problem will disappear. Then, you can move on to the next item on your list.

10.3

It is also possible that you will have several different types of problems. In this case, divide your list based on the most appropriate time in the writing process for you to apply the focusing exercise. For example, content and organization mistakes usually are handled best at the revision stage of writing, mechanics at the proofreading stage, and style at both the revision and proofreading stages.

You don't want to focus on more than one thing at a time, but your writing program could be separated according to the different steps in the writing process.

My Personal Writing Program

Revision:

1. Make sure the most important idea is at the beginning of the writing.

2. Include only information the reader needs to make a decision.

Proofreading:

1. Combine sentences so that important ideas are emphasized.

2. Review parallel structure in the document.

3. Review vague pronouns. Make sure that my reader knows what the pronoun stands for.

Remember, too, that your personal writing program might deal with a problem that we have not mentioned here. You can be as creative as you want. In the following example, the supervisor of the writer complained that the writer never paused between composing and submitting the document. The writer thought about it and came up with this program:

My Personal Writing Program

1. When I complete a document, I will read it through once pretending that I am the designated reader. I will ask myself, "If I were the reader, would I understand this document? Would I be overwhelmed by too much information? Would I have questions?" I will revise my work based on my answers.

2. When I have finished the first revision, I will let my document sit for at least an hour (24 hours is better).

3. As I start the second revision, I will read the document again asking myself the questions in #1 and then will revise accordingly. If I have time, I will put the document aside again for at least an hour.

4. Before turning in the document, I will proof it line by line using a nontransparent ruler. I will concentrate on the following errors, one at a time.

   A. Non-agreement of subjects and verbs

   B. Sentence fragments

   C. Repetitive vocabulary

One last point. Even with a personal writing program, your writing won't change overnight. Good writing, we said at the beginning of this book, is good thinking. Stick to the writing program, and you will find that your writing will become more successful from draft to draft and from document to document.

PREPARING YOUR PERSONAL WRITING PROGRAM:
A DIAGNOSTIC CHECKLIST

SYMPTOM	DIAGNOSIS
Content	
The writing is returned with comments that suggest the writer has missed the point.	The assignment was not understood.
The writing is returned with large sections crossed out.	There is too much information.
The writing is returned with questions about the content.	There is not enough information.
Organization	
The comments on the work say it "doesn't flow," "jumps around a lot," or "doesn't make sense."	The organization is poor.

TREATMENT

Before beginning any important writing project, put the assignment in writing. Include the subject, purpose, the reader or audience, the required length, and, if necessary, the format and due date.

Review the purpose statement. Cross out information which doesn't support the purpose and rewrite.

Practice role playing. Put aside your document for at least an hour. When you pick it up again, read it critically as if you were the intended audience. Ask yourself, "As the reader, would I be persuaded to do what this document wants me to do? Is there enough information to decide? Is there enough information for me to respond easily? Do I feel satisfied with the message?" Revise your work based on your answers.

Outline. For letters or memos, use the outlines suggested in Chapter 2. For longer documents use an appropriate pattern from Chapter 3.

WRITING PROGRAM CHECKLIST (cont.)

SYMPTOM	DIAGNOSIS
Mechanics	
Margins are corrected.	Formatting is incorrect.
Spelling is corrected.	Poor spelling.
Grammar or punctuation is corrected.	Incorrect grammar and punctuation.
Style	
The comments indicate that writing is either too formal or informal for the audience.	The tone needs to be adjusted.
The comments on the draft indicate that some ideas should be phrased stronger.	The sentence emphasis is weak or incorrect.
The comments on the writing suggest it doesn't "sound" professional.	The phrasing does not use the acceptable standard of the profession.

TREATMENT

Make and use a style sheet.

Buy a book which includes a spelling program. Run all documents through a computer spell check.

Make a list of all the errors in your writing. Review it concentrating only on the most common error. Work through each of your documents in this way until the problem disappears. Use a computer grammar check. Proofread carefully.

Role play: pretend that the reader is someone you don't know very well. Rewrite, implementing an appropriate tone.

Combine ideas and rewrite so that the main ideas are in the main parts of the sentence and the subordinate ideas are in the subordinate parts of the sentence.

Determine who are the good writers in your organization. Imitate their style.

Index

179